HELLO!™
W🏛SHINGT🌐N

a handbook on everyday living
for international residents

7701 Woodmont Avenue #1108
Bethesda, Maryland 20814
301/913-0074

Published by Hello! America, Inc.
7701 Woodmont Avenue #1108 Bethesda, Maryland 20814 301/913-0074

Hello! America, Inc. acknowledges Presentation Task Force as the primary source of graphic images in this publication. The copyright owner of these images is New Vision Technologies, Inc.

Brand name products mentioned in this publication are proprietary property of the applicable firm, subject to trademark protection, and registered with government offices.

While the Publisher has made every reasonable attempt to obtain accurate information and verify same, occasional errors are inevitable due to the magnitude of the data base. All prices and costs are estimates and are subject to change. Should you discover any error, please write the publisher so that corrections may be entered in future editions.

The appearance of listing anywhere in this publication does not constitute an endorsement from the publisher.

Manufactured in the United States of America.

ISBN:0-9635633-0-0

Acknowledgements

Author and Publisher: Judy Priven

Business Development: Lew Priven

Associate Publisher: Amy Kossoff

Book Design: Jesse Guerra

Editors: Deborah Becker Cotto, Nisi Hamilton, Laura Richardson, Nora Thapa

Desktop Publishing & Artwork: Lorie Frishman, Jesse Guerra, Kate Reilly

Distribution: Judith Harley, Amy Kossoff

Marketing: Marti Campbell, Amy Kossoff

Special Projects: Lorie Frishman

Advertising Sales: Judith Harley, Amy Kossoff, Nisi Hamilton

Cover Design: Don Dailey (Dailey Direct), John Thompson (Direct Design)

Research: Pat Asleson, Sara Cherner, Deborah Becker Cotto, Nisi Hamilton, Laura Richardson

Publications Consulting: Alma Lopez (Compu-Pub)

Special thanks to Deize Walker for overall support and encouragement.

Bank on it worldwide.

CITIBANK®

5708 5312 3456 7891

ONE CARD LETS YOU MANAGE YOUR MONEY OVERSEAS AS EASILY AS IF YOU'RE ACROSS TOWN.

When Citibank is your bank, the whole world is your neighborhood. Because now there are Citicard Banking Center® locations around the world that make you feel like you never left home.

Look up your balances in dollars. Get cash in local currency at competitive exchange rates. Move and manage your money right on the screen, 24 hours a day, in English or up to nine other languages. Whether you're in Spain, Germany, Greece, Singapore, Belgium or Hong Kong. Of course, any Citicard Banking Center also lets you get cash and check account balances. Plus, 80,000 CIRRUS® ATMs in 27 countries give you worldwide access to cash, too.

BANKING IS AS EASY IN SINGAPORE AS IT IS IN SILVER SPRING

To find out more, call CitiPhone Banking℠ at **(202) 857-6700** (or **1-800-926-1067** outside the D.C. Metro area). You won't find another bank in the world like it.

THE **CITI** NEVER SLEEPS®

CITIBANK®

Table of Contents

Preface

. *How to use "Hello! Washington"* . *the Washington metro area*
. *in an emergency* . *staying safe*

How to Use
__Hello!™ Washington__

First Pages

In an Emergency: what to do and say.   **Staying Safe:** basic rules for staying safe.

Chapters

Chapter openers: maps; pictures of everyday objects and forms.
Chapter text: American customs and ways of doing things.

1,2,3... step-by-step directions

(what you should do first, second...and last)

 important ideas

 documents or papers you need

 answers to questions you might ask

 time to start

 warning
(what *not* to do; what to watch out for)

 cost

"Information": telephone numbers and addresses.
"Words to Know": American words used in everyday life.
Advertisements: Messages from stores and services you need.**

Appendix

Holidays, climate, money, conversions, and books to read about the Washington area

---

* The costs on these pages are good for the spring of 1993. Many of these costs may be higher in a short time. Other costs are estimates; they are not exact. Be sure to find out for yourself how much to pay.
** The Publisher is not responsible for any actions or advice given by the stores and services listed here.

The Washington Metro Area

Montgomery County

• Gaithersburg

• Rockville

Takoma Park •

• Greenbelt
• College Park

Bowie •

Arlington County

Falls • Church

DC

Fairfax •

Alexandria •

Prince George's County

Fairfax County

Compared with other American metro areas, Washington has:

- the highest % of workers with executive and managerial jobs. **20.0%**

- the highest median household income. **$47,254**

- the second longest commuting time. **29.5 minutes**

- the highest % of people 25 and older with a graduate or professional degree. **16.6%**

- about the same % of people who speak a foreign language at home. **14.7%**

- the highest % of working women. **68.8%**

___In an Emergency___

Call 911

Fire

1. **Call:** 911

2. **Say:**

- "I would like to report a fire."
- "Please come to... (your address)."

3. **Tell**:
- which room the fire is in.
- how big the fire is.
- how the fire started.

Medical Emergency

1. **Call:** 911

2. **Say:**

- "I need an ambulance right away."
- "Please come to... (your address)."

3. **Answer questions** about the accident or sickness.

Crime

1. **Call:** 911. Call if:
- you think someone is committing a crime—*do not wait* until a crime has happened.

2. **Say:**

- "I would like to report a (break-in, mugging, or other crime.)"
- "Please come to ...(your address)."

3. **Answer questions** about the crime.

Help will come in 5-10 minutes.

Staying Safe

Your pocketbook or wallet

- **Always** keep your wallet or pocketbook with you. Strap your pocketbook across your shoulder if you can.
- **Always** keep your pocketbook closed, with the locks facing you.
- **Always** keep your wallet inside your jacket pocket.

Your credit cards

- **Always** call the company right away if your card is lost or stolen.
- **Always** keep the number of your credit card at home.
- **Always** tear up the black carbon paper into little pieces.

Your money

- **Never** carry large amounts of cash. Carry a credit card or checks instead.
- **Never** count out large amounts of money where others can see you.

The Metro

Usually, the Metro is safe—even late at night. But:

- **Always** check the area outside the Metro before you go there at night.
- **Always** stand with other people in the station.
- **Always** stand away from the edge of the platform.
- **Never** pay attention to people who are arguing loudly; their partner may try to steal your wallet.

In your home

- **Always** make sure the area is safe at night before you buy or rent a home (see chapter on "Finding a New Home").
- **Always** lock your doors and windows. Most people have double locks, or locks that close two times.
- **Never** leave valuables near an open window.

Your children

Most people who kidnap children are not strangers—they are divorced or separated parents. But tell your children:

- **Always** dial 911 in an emergency.
- **Never** talk to or get into a car with strangers.
- **Never** let strangers into your home if they are alone.
- **Never** tell a stranger on the phone that they are alone. (Tell them to say you "cannot come to the phone.")

Your car

- **Always** keep the doors locked—when you are driving or leaving the car.
- **Always** put your luggage, tapes, and other valuables in the trunk *before* you reach the parking lot. (If you put your valuables in the trunk and walk away, someone may see you and get into the trunk.)
- **Always** carry a copy of your car registration papers in your wallet. Show these papers to the police if someone steals your car.
- **Always** have your key ready as you walk toward the car. Look inside quickly; then open the door and get in.
- **Never** leave the keys in the car.
- **Never** let strangers in the car.

At the bank machine

- **Always** be sure no one can grab you when you are using the machine.
- **Always** look around before you open the door or use the machine.

In a hotel

- **Always** keep your valuables in the hotel safe.
- **Never** leave valuables in the room when you are gone.

Before You Come

Money

Cash in U.S. dollars

Traveler's checks
in U.S. dollars

Credit cards

Documents

Entry papers

Financial history/
bank routing information

Medical history/
medicine prescriptions

Birth certificate

Driving history and
auto information

Education records
and diplomas

What to Bring

Money

- cash in U.S. dollars. Bring U.S. $150-$200 in cash for things you will need right away—for example, a taxi from the airport or food. If you arrive on a weekend, you may want to bring $100 more, since most banks in the area are closed.
- traveler's checks. Issued in U.S. dollars, these can be used as cash; if they are lost or stolen, you will get new ones.
- credit cards. Get an American Express or Diner's Club card before you leave. These are most likely to issue you an American card after you get here (see chapter on "Money Matters").

Documents

Entry papers.

- a passport for each family member 21 years or older. Check the expiration date on your passport(s); if it expires less than 6 months from the time you plan to enter the U.S., ask for an extension. Keep your passport valid at all times.
- a visa for each family member 21 years or older. This is stamped on the inside of your passport at the U.S. Consulate. The visa tells
  - the purpose of your visit.
  - the expiration date, or last date, you can enter the U.S.
  - how many times you can enter (see chapter on "Your Legal Status").

One family member has the visa status of "principal employee" or "principal student." Other family members have "derivative status."

Financial information.

- copy of your latest tax returns.
- proof that you own your home in your country.
- bank statements and records of any other assets.
- credit or loan documents.
- bank information. To transfer money to the U.S., you will need your bank's
  - routing number (American Bank Association).
  - address.
  - account number (see chapter on "Money Matters").

Automobile information.

- International Driver's License or your current driver's license.
- "no claim letter" (in English) from your car insurance company, showing that you are a safe driver. This letter may reduce your car insurance payments in the U.S.
- car ownership records if you are bringing your car to the U.S., including your
  - bill of sale.
  - international registration marker.
  - car serial and motor numbers.
  - insurance policy records.

Medical records.

- immunizations.
- medicines you take.
- illnesses you have had.

Birth certificates. Bring originals (preferably translated into English and notarized).

Education records.

- transcripts.
- diplomas.
- test records (such as the TOEFL).

Job and professional records.

- reference letters (on company or university stationery).
- your résumé.
- proof of your qualifications (see chapter on "Finding Work").

Legal papers.

- copies of will(s).
- proof of legal guardianship for any minor (child under the age of 18) who is accompanying you and is not your own child.

Copies of insurance policies.

Compare the cost of extending your current health insurance coverage versus purchasing coverage in the U.S.

Inventory.

List all items packed, shipped, or stored.

Useful items

You may want:

- an extra pair of prescription eyeglasses.
- a thermometer for measuring degrees Celsius.
- household medicine and antibiotics. In the U.S., you will need a prescription for many medicines (see chapter on "Medical Care"). Check with the U.S. Consulate in your area about restrictions on bringing drugs to the U.S. (see chapter on "Your Legal Status").
- extra photographs (headshots). The photos should be passport size. You need these for the many forms you will complete.
- extra luggage keys.

What to leave at home

Compare the cost of shipping or bringing an item versus buying it in the U.S. For example, compare:

- large items—such as furniture.
- everyday items—such as medicines, shoes, or clothing.

Clothing.

- heavy indoor clothing. Almost all homes and buildings have air conditioning and central heating, so temperatures indoors are about the same throughout the year.
- extra children's clothing. Children who move to the U.S. often want what American

5

children wear; since clothing in the U.S. is often cheap, you may want to buy it here.

Large household items.

- appliances. The electrical outlets and currents here are different from those in most countries. The U.S. electricity standard is 110-120 volt, 60 cycles AC. Before you come, be sure any appliances you bring will work here.
- furniture. Consider buying your furniture here. Furniture is usually cheaper in the U.S.—especially used furniture (see chapter on "Moving In").

Legal Matters

Bringing items into the U.S.

Ask the U.S. Consulate nearest you about bringing:

Items from certain countries. You cannot import some items from Cambodia, Cuba, North Korea, or Vietnam.

Items needing a special permit.

- firearms and ammunition.
- some drugs and medicines.
- plants and meat products, such as fruits, vegetables, and seeds, and untanned animal furs or skins.

Gold coins, jewelry, and medals. You can import only a certain amount of these items.

Cars. Any car brought into the U.S. must meet U.S. highway safety standards and have a working catalytic converter. You will also need specific automobile documents (see "What to Bring").

Pets.

- Have your pet examined by a veterinarian. U.S. Customs will not admit a pet that has any diseases it can transmit to humans. If you have a dog or cat, bring a health certificate from the veterinarian.
- Have dogs or cats 3 months or older vaccinated against rabies at least 30 days before coming to the U.S.
- Check the hours of operation at your port of arrival to be sure that an officer is available to inspect your pet when you arrive at U.S. Customs.
- Make plans with the airline for shipping your pet. Ask which kind of pet carrier you need.
- Label all pet carriers with
  - your name and address in the U.S.
  - the name and address of anyone who will be picking up your pet.
  - a statement with the number of animals contained in each shipment.
- Check to be sure your hotel or housing allows pets.

Taking items back into your country

Procedures and regulations. Be sure you know about any special procedures, restrictions, or taxes on taking possessions (such as a car) into your own country from the U.S.

If necessary, save receipts or proofs of purchase for anything you may have difficulty taking back into your country. These may include:

- cars.
- cameras.
- jewelry.

Special problems. Be sure any appliances or electrical equipment purchased in the U.S. will work in your home country.

Words to Know

Antibiotic: a kind of medicine—for example, medicine for sore throats and other infections

Assets: the property and money a person has

Bank statement: a record of how much money you have in your bank account

Bill of sale: a paper that shows what you bought and how much you paid

Birth certificate: an official document that shows when and where a person was born

Car serial number: the identification number of a car—often on the dashboard or under the hood

Central heating: a heating system that heats the whole house—not just one room

Derivative status: the legal status for families of the principal student or employee

Expiration date: the date your visa ends

Extension: getting permission to stay longer

Firearms: guns and other weapons that fire

Guardianship: having the legal responsibility to care for a child

Immunization: medicine or injection that keeps you from getting diseases

Inventory: a list of all items packed, shipped, or stored

No claim letter: a letter from your car insurance company that shows you are a safe driver

Pet carrier: a strong box that holds pets while traveling

Principal employee: the employee who holds the visa for himself or herself and for the family

Principal student: the student who holds the visa for himself or herself and for the family

Qualification: the ability to do a job

Reference letter: a letter from your past employer that says you did a good job

Routing number: a bank's identification number for international wire transfers; a bank's electronic address

Tax return: a document you send to the government each year. It shows how much money you made and the taxes you paid.

Transcript: a person's official school record that shows the classes taken and the grades received

Vaccinated: having a shot (see "Immunization")

Will: an official document that shows who gets a person's money and property after he or she dies

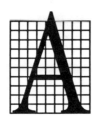

__When You Arrive__

Baltimore-Washington International

301/261-1000
To DC (Union Station):
35mi/56km
45min-1hr
Taxi: $40-$55

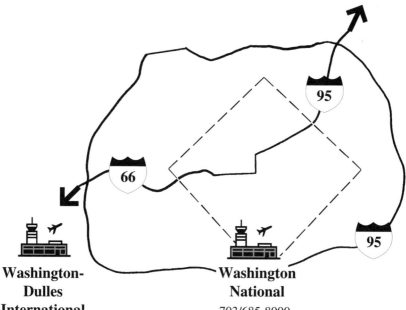

**Washington-
Dulles
International**

703/661-2700
To DC (Union Station):
28mi/44.8km
35-40 minutes
Taxi: $40-50

**Washington
National**

703/685-8000
To DC (Union Station):
10mi/16km
20-25 minutes
Taxi: about $15

At the Airport

Washington's airports

The Washington area has three major airports:

- Washington-Dulles International Airport (international and domestic flights).
- Washington National Airport (domestic flights only).
- Baltimore-Washington International (BWI) Airport (international and domestic flights).

For more information on these airports, see this chapter's page opener and "Information" section.

Entering the U.S.

When your enter the U.S., you will need to show the immigration officer your:

- passport.
- visa, which is stamped inside your passport.
- I-94 card. The officer will attach this to your passport. Check to see how long you are permitted to stay in the U.S. If you need to stay longer, explain why you are coming to the U.S. and ask for an extension. Do not remove the card after you leave the airport.
- U.S. Customs declaration card.
- entry papers—such as the IAP-66 ("pink") form.

How to enter the U.S.

1. **Be sure your I-94 and U.S. customs declaration cards are completed correctly.**

You will receive these cards on the airplane before you arrive.

2. **Go through immigration.**

Give the immigration officer your papers.

3. **Follow the signs to the baggage claim area.**

4. **Stop at a customs inspection station.**

If you have any pets or plants, stop at the U.S. Department of Agriculture (USDA) inspection station.

5. **Exchange money.**

You should have $150-$200 cash with you when you leave the airport.

Make copies of all your papers after you arrive—in case any of these papers get lost.

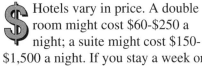

Arrival assistance

The Traveler's Aid Society (TAS) has a desk at all the Washington airports. It is open 24 hours a day and helps with problems such as money and transportation.

Transportation

All three major airports have public transportation to downtown Washington (see "Information" and this chapter's opener for costs). Depending on the airport, you can take a:

- taxi. In addition to the fare, the taxi charges $1-$1.25 for each extra passenger. You will also have to pay about 50¢ for each piece of baggage. Tip the driver about 15% of the fare.
- limousine.
- bus.
- train, either the Metrorail or MARC (commuter rail).
- rental car (see chapter on "Traveling").

Where to Stay

Hotels

Most hotels have:

- maid service.
- laundry service.
- room service.
- dining.

Some hotels offer:

- suites with small kitchens.
- free parking.

- bilingual staff members (see chapter on "Traveling").

 Hotels vary in price. A double room might cost $60-$250 a night; a suite might cost $150-$1,500 a night. If you stay a week or longer, ask about special long-term rates. Daily rates are more expensive.

Guest houses

You may rent a room at a guest house, for long- or short-term. Usually, you share a bathroom with other guests. Some offer meals.

The average cost of one room is $20-$35 a night, per person.

Temporary homes

You can rent a temporary home for 1 week, 1 month, or more. Most temporary homes come with everything you need—such as furniture, linens (sheets and towels), bedding, dishes, kitchen utensils, and appliances (see chapter on "Finding a New Home" for information on what to look for in a home).

In general, furnished apartments cost about 50% more than unfurnished apartments. Some sample costs for furnished apartments are:

- efficiency (studio apartment). $30-$50 a day; $800-$1,500 a month.
- two-bedroom. $40-$70 a day; $1,200-$2,000 a month.

13

You will pay a security deposit (about 1 month's rent) along with the first rent payment; you will get the money back when you leave. Find out which fees and services are included in the price.

Services. Some short-term places offer special services that may be included in the rental price. For example, you may get:

- 24-hour desk or concierge service.
- maid service.
- activities programs.
- newspaper delivery.
- transportation to and from airports.

Pet rules. If you have a pet, be sure it can stay with you.

Social Security

 Employers, banks, and schools use the Social Security card for identification. You may not need a card if you are a:

- dependent.
- diplomat.

Some dependents need a Social Security card if they get a job or go to college.

If you can work, your Social Security card will say, "Authorized to be Employed." Your employer should also check your other documents to be sure.

To get a Social Security card, go to the nearest Social Security office in person (see "Information"). Take:

- your passport with the I-94 card.
- immigration papers—such as the IAP-66 (pink) form.
- completed SS-5 application form. You can get one at the Social Security office.

How to begin

1. Ask your employer or school for help.

2. Have all official documents translated into English.

All translations should be notarized by a notary public or authenticated by your country's embassy. You will pay a small fee—usually $2-$3. You must show some form of identification—such as a driver's license or a passport. You can find a notary public at:

- banks.
- law offices.
- most real estate offices.
- some translation companies.

3. Apply for a Social Security card.

4. Open a bank account (see chapter on "Money Matters").

Rent a safety deposit box for all valuables.

Getting Settled

Once you have taken care of your immediate needs, you should:

- register your child(ren) at a school (see chapter on "Your Older Child").
- get a driver's license (see chapter on "Driving a Car").
- get insurance for
  - your car.
  - health care (see chapter on "Medical Care").
  - personal property (see chapter on "Moving In").
- make a list of emergency telephone numbers—for example, fire, police, and hospitals (see "In an Emergency" at the beginning of the book).
- find a family doctor (see chapter on "Medical Care").
- arrange for visa extensions or work permission for dependents (see chapter on "Your Legal Status").

Who Can Help

Traveler's bureaus

Traveler's bureaus provide information on accommodations, sightseeing, restaurants, and shopping (see "Information").

Orientation programs

Orientation programs can help you:

- become familiar with the area.
- learn about American culture.
- deal with culture shock.
- solve general problems.

Your employer or school may have an orientation program (see "Information").

Traveler's bureaus

Traveler's Aid Society of Washington (TAS):

- Dulles Airport: 703/661-8636
- National Airport: 703/684-3472
- Union Station: 202/546-3120

The International Visitors Information Service (IVIS): in addition to walk-in service, this office also gives help by telephone in 45 languages. 202/939-5566

The Washington Convention & Visitors Information Center: 202/789-7038

Orientation programs

Hello! America: 301/913-0074

Meridian International Center: 202/667-6800

Foreign Student Service Council of Greater Washington: 202/232-4979

Information

Airports

Baltimore-Washington International Airport, MD.

General information: 301/261-1000

Airport Connection bus: 7 am-10 pm; $14 one way to 1517 K St., NW, Washington, DC. 301/261-1091 or 1-410/859-7545

MARC train (commuter rail): 6:30 am-9:45 pm, Monday-Friday; $4.25 one way to Washington's Union Station. 1-800/325-7245

Parking: 1-410/859-9230

Washington-Dulles International Airport, VA.

General information: 703/661-2700

Dulles Express bus: $8 one way to West Falls Church Metro station

Washington Flyer bus: 6 am-11 pm; $14 one way to 1517 K St., NW, Washington, DC; by reservation only. 703/685-1400

Taxi service: 703/661-8230

Parking: 703/661-5746

Washington National Airport, VA.

General information: 703/685-8000

Washington Flyer bus: $8 one way to 1517 K St., NW, Washington, DC; by reservation only. 703/685-1400

Metro (blue/yellow lines): 202/637-7000

Parking: 703/271-4311

U.S. Government offices

Immigration and Naturalization Service (INS) Alien Information.

- DC and VA: 202/307-1501
- MD: 1-410/962-2065

U.S. Customs Service.

- Main office: 202/927-2095
- Customs Entry Control, Dulles Airport: 703/661-8281

Social Security: 1-800/772-1213

DC

- 2100 M St., NW.
- 3005 Bladensburg Rd., NE.
- 333 Hawaii Ave., NE.
- 3244 Pennsylvania Ave., SE.

MD

- 51 Monroe St. (lower level), Rockville.
- 11160 Veirs Mill Rd., Wheaton.
- 6400 Old Branch Ave., Camp Springs.
- 7701 Greenbelt Rd., Greenbelt.
- 71 Yost Place, Seat Pleasant.

VA

- 9108 Mathis Ave., Manassas.
- 7777 Leesburg Pike, Falls Church.
- 2300 South 9th St., Arlington.
- 206 N. Washington St., Alexandria.

Words to Know

Authenticate: to stamp a document to show it is true

Bilingual: speaking two languages

Concierge: a person who works at the front desk of a hotel or apartment building

Customs inspection station: the place at the airport where officers see what is in your baggage

Customs declaration card: a card you get on the airplane. You write what you are bringing into the U.S.

Domestic flight: an airline flight inside the U.S.—not international

Extension: a written agreement that lets you stay in the country longer

Guest house: a house where you can rent a room for a short or long time

I-94 card: a card that an immigration officer attaches to your passport

Limousine: a large car, also called a "limo"

Notarize: to make a document legal; to put an official stamp on a document

Notary public: a person who makes a document legal

Orientation program: a service for newcomers

Security deposit: the money you pay the owner of the house or apartment before you rent it

Social Security card: a U.S. government card with an identification number—needed to work legally in the U.S.

Suite: a group of rooms in a hotel

Temporary home: a house you can rent for a short or long time

Traveler's Aid Society (TAS): a place at the airport that helps travelers

Smart Money Buys
The Guide Before You Move.

The New Settler's Guide for Washington can make your next move your smartest move.

The Guide is the only available relocation handbook that compares the entire Washington metropolitan area community by community.

It is exclusively designed for newcomers and not only covers Washington, D.C. but 16 of the surrounding counties in nearby Maryland and Virginia and 90 individual communities. It will give you ranges on apartments, condo's and single family homes; the type of community; travel time to Washington; schools; taxes; recreation; transportation and much more. The Guide also has several maps and over 168 pages.

Before you move, order The New Settler's Guide for $9.00 (includes postage and handling). Send your address and $9.00 check or money order to:
The New Settler's Guide • Harrison Duke
8824 Tuckerman Lane • Potomac, MD 20854 • (301) 299-7507

THE VIRGINIAN

Your answer to convenience and comfort without the cost.

Rates Starting

from $45⁰⁰ per day

- Fully furnished efficiency, one and two bedroom apartments
- Maid service included every other day
- Free parking
- Complimentary cable television with HBO
- Free local phone calls
- Free metro shuttle service to the Rosslyn metro
- Complimentary Continental Breakfast
- State of the art exercise facility
- 24 hour message service & security
- Outdoor pool and sundeck
- Men's and Women's sauna
- Same day laundry & valet service
- Coin operated laundry facility
- Pets welcome

"Hotel Convenience with Residential Comfort"
1500 Arlington Boulevard
Arlington, VA 22209
(703) 522-9600 • (800) 275-2866
FAX (202) 525-4462

Tired of living in a Hotel?

CORPORATE APARTMENT HOMES
Northern Va. ● Maryland ● D.C.

- Completely furnished and accessorized
- Phone service, utilities, washer/dryer included
- Maid service available
- Fitness center, pools, tennis and racquetball courts included
- Short term rentals, 2 weeks plus at select locations

**Luxury Accommodations
at half the cost!**

Corporate
and
Executive
TEMPORARY
HOUSING
INC.
Serving
Northern Virginia

1-800-933-8367

Fax: 703-329-8659
Our service begins the day you call.

18

_____Social Security Card_____

SOCIAL SECURITY

000-86-4485

THIS NUMBER HAS BEEN ESTABLISHED FOR

John Edgar Doe

SIGNATURE

Your Legal Status

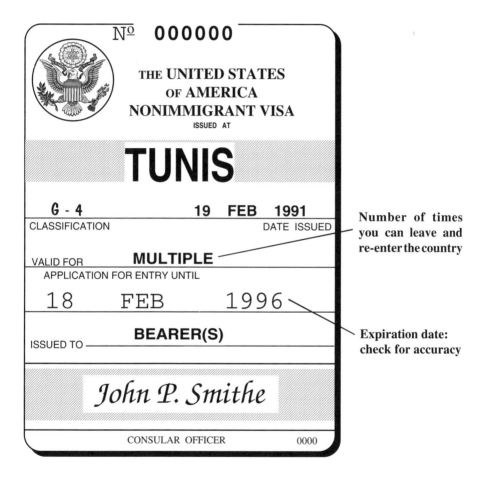

Nº 000000

THE **UNITED STATES**
OF **AMERICA**
NONIMMIGRANT VISA
ISSUED AT

TUNIS

G - 4   19   FEB   1991

CLASSIFICATION   DATE ISSUED

VALID FOR   **MULTIPLE**

APPLICATION FOR ENTRY UNTIL

18   FEB   1996

BEARER(S)

ISSUED TO

John P. Smithe

CONSULAR OFFICER   0000

Number of times you can leave and re-enter the country

Expiration date: check for accuracy

What Your Visa Means

Your visa. Your visa lets you enter the U.S. and shows:

- whether you can work (see chapter on "Finding Work").
- the number of years you can stay. This number varies according to the country of origin.
- the number of times you can leave the U.S. and come back again. This varies according to the country of origin and type of visa. To find out how many times you can leave, call the U.S. Embassy or Consulate in your home city.
- what kind of work or studies you are doing.

Other papers. To find out about other papers you need, see chapters on "Before You Come" and "When You Arrive."

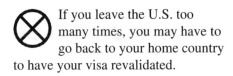 If you leave the U.S. too many times, you may have to go back to your home country to have your visa revalidated.

Avoiding Common Problems

How to plan ahead

1. **Check your papers.**

Be sure they are filled out correctly (see chapter on "Before You Come"). If you find an error—for example, an incorrect date—you may want to see an attorney right away.

2. **Keep a calendar of the important dates.**

For example, write the dates when you:

Remember that everyone's papers and problems are different. Your friends may have solved their problems in a short time, but your problem may take a lot longer.

Correcting errors or changing your status can be frustrating; you may wait a long time and make many phone calls. Remember, too, that INS officials do not care about your personal wealth or position. To persuade these officials to help you, tell them why your work here is important.

- are leaving the country.
- need an extension.
- are changing your status.

Also write the dates when you should see an attorney or contact the Immigration and Naturalization Service (INS). This will save you a lot of time.

3. **See an attorney about 3 months after you arrive—even if you think you have no problems.**

The attorney will talk about your future plans and look over your visa (see "Choosing an Attorney"). Many attorneys will give you a free first visit.

Common problems

 Changing your visa may take 2 months or a year; every case is different. To be safe, begin as soon as you know about a problem or a possible change.

Errors on visa/papers (see "How to plan ahead").

Changes in status. Find out what to do if:

- you are changing jobs. Check with an attorney or other professional, even if you will be working for the same employer. For example, exchange visitors may have to fill out some forms to change from research to clinical work.

- you are changing schools. Go to the school's international office or the person in charge of the I-20 process at your new school.
- you are finishing your studies and going to work.
- you are getting married or divorced.

Extensions. Getting an extension often takes about 30-45 days, with a grace period of about 240 days as soon as you file; that is, you have 240 days after you file to get your extension approved. But special problems can cause the process to take longer or the grace period to be delayed. Start *at least* 3 months ahead of time.

Choosing an Attorney

Attorneys. To find an attorney:

- Ask your embassy for recommendations.
- Call the American Immigration Lawyers Association (see "Information").
- Talk to an attorney before you hire him or her. Again, many attorneys will talk to you in person for free at your first visit.

Visa services. Before you choose a visa service, ask:

- how much the service charges.
- what the service will do.
- how long the service has been in business.

Also ask for the names of references you can call.

Some visa services charge a lot of money for doing some thing you can do on your own. Others have been charged with fraud or illegal practices. Be careful when choosing a service!

Information

American Immigration Lawyers Association: 202/371-9377

Words to Know

American Immigration Lawyers Association: a group that represents lawyers who practice immigration law

Attorney: a person who represents you in business and law

Exchange visitor program: a program in which two people from different countries trade jobs

Extension: a written agreement that allows more time to be in the country after a visa runs out

Fraud: a dishonest act, usually in business or law

Immigration and Naturalization Service (INS): the U.S. government agency responsible for monitoring who comes into the country and how long they can stay

Washington on $5 a Day.

Go anywhere Metrorail goes with the all new
Metrorail One Day Pass. Ride from 9:30 a.m.
till closing on weekdays, or all day long on
weekends and federal holidays. It's just $5
at Metro Center, the Pentagon, Metro
Headquarters, most Safeway and Giant stores,
Crystal City Commuter Center, the Ballston
Transit Store and selected MARC Rail stations.
Because now more than ever, the more you
ride, the more you save.

__Getting Around__

Metrobus Token

(sold at any Metro sales office, some banks, and supermarkets)

1 token	$1.00
10 tokens	$9.00
20 tokens	$18.00

Metrorail Farecard
(sold at any Metro station)

Put card in this way

How much you paid

How much your
farecard is
worth now

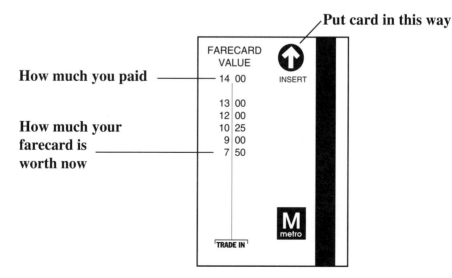

METRORAIL SYSTEM MAP

Legend

- Red Line - Wheaton/Shady Grove
- Blue Line - Addison Road/Van Dorn Street
- Orange Line - New Carrollton/Vienna
- Yellow Line - Mt. Vernon Sq-UDC/Huntington
- Green Line - U Street-Cardozo/Anacostia

Smoking is not permitted on escalators, elevators, in stations, trains or buses.

Virginia Railway Express
MARC Commuter Rail Services
All day Parking
Transfer Station
Station in service
Future Station

The Metro System

 The Metro is the public transportation system that goes through the Washington Metropolitan area (see "The Metrorail System Map" at the beginning of the chapter). It has:

- a train system, sometimes called the "Metrorail system" or just "the Metro." Most of the trains are underground.
- buses, which connect with the trains. These are called "Metrobuses."

Some cities and counties also have their own buses that connect with the Metro system.

 Some buses come every 10 minutes, but others come only once an hour. Some buses do not run on weekends and holidays. You can find free schedules in all Metro stations and on Metrobuses. You can also call Metrobus for individual schedules.

The Metrorail runs every 5 minutes during peak hours and every 10-12 minutes at other times (see "Information" for hours of operation).

Peak hours—when the costs are higher—are:

- 5:30-9:30 am.
- 3-7 pm.

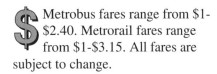 Metrobus fares range from $1-$2.40. Metrorail fares range from $1-$3.15. All fares are subject to change.

Discounts

Some people get discounts—for example, senior citizens (people over 65 years old).

Flashpasses

The Metro has many kinds of flashpasses. One flashpass is good for 2 weeks; you can use the Metrorail or Metrobus as many times as you want. The cost is $50.

Choose the pass that is best for you. You may buy one at any Metro office or in many stores or banks. Call the Metro office to find out which place is closest to you (see "Information").

Metrorail (the Metro)

Stations

Metro stations have tall brown columns with a large "M" at the top. Inside, every Metrorail station has:

- two maps, showing
  - the overall routes.
  - the streets in the area of the station.
- a fare chart. The chart tells
  - the cost to go from one station to another.

- the time it takes to go from one station to another.
- the route you are taking.
- a farecard machine. Use this machine to buy your farecard (see "The farecard").
- signs and posts telling you where to go.
- a transfer machine. Transfer machines are usually right near the escalator going down to the rails. Get a transfer slip if
  - you will be using a bus after the subway ride.
  - your car is in a Metro parking lot. You may need to show the slip to an attendant.

The farecard. You can use the farecard for more than one trip. Each time you use the farecard, the cost of the trip is subtracted, or taken away, from the amount shown (see this chapter's opener).

You can buy the farecard from the machine inside any Metro station. If you buy a farecard for $10 or more, a 5% bonus is added to your card.

Directions for getting a farecard are on the machine. All machines take $1 or $5 bills; some also take $10 or $20 bills. The machine gives change, but all the change is in quarters (25¢ coins). For example, if you ask for $2 in change, you will get eight quarters.

Parking. Some stations have parking lots.

Kiss & Ride. To drop someone off, drive to this area; the area is called "Kiss & Ride" because someone can drive you to the station and kiss you goodbye.

Some Kiss & Ride areas may have a few parking spaces; these spaces are often filled.

How to ride the Metro

1. **Read the fare chart.**
Remember the last stop on the route so you will get on the right train.

2. **Ask directions.**
The person at the booth can tell you which route you want. If you do not know English well, look at the map near the farecard machine and near the rails.

3. **Get a farecard.**
The machines are near the entrance to the station.

4. **Put the farecard in the slot with the green arrow and go through the gate.** (The card will be returned.)

5. **Get a transfer slip near the escalators.**

6. **Look at the maps near the tracks.**

7. **Get on the train.**

8. **Transfer to another line if necessary.**

9. **Choose the right exit.**

You may ask the person in the booth or look at the station map of the neighborhood.

10. **Put the card in the slot with the green arrow and go through the gate.**

The amount of the fare is subtracted. (The card will not be returned if it was for the exact amount of the fare.)

11. **Add money to your card if necessary.**

If the gate stays closed when you put your card in, you need to add money to your card. Use the EXITFARE machine; it tells how much money to put in.

Metrobus

Metrobus stops have tall red, white, and blue striped signs. The list of buses stopping there is sometimes on the sign.

You need the exact change or tokens; find out about how much the trip costs ahead of time. To be safe, take two tokens and about $1 in change for each way.

The fare is:

DC: $1.

MD:

- within MD: $1.
- from DC to MD: $1.65-$1.90.

Riders in Montgomery County can buy an all-day pass for $1.50 after 9:30 am on weekdays and all day on weekends.

VA:

- non-peak hours: $1.
- peak hours: up to $2.05.
- from DC to VA: up to $2.40.

Bus to bus

Transfers. Transfers are free. They are good for 2 hours and for only one direction.

- bus to bus. Ask the driver for a transfer when you pay your fare.
- bus to subway. You cannot get a transfer from a bus to a subway.
- subway to bus. Get your transfer slip while you are still in the subway station. You may have to pay a small fee when you get on the bus.

Suburban Buses

Bus prices are different for each route. Fares range from 35¢ for the Fairfax CUE to $1 for others during peak hours. Transfers cost extra.

The Ride-On goes in Montgomery County, MD. The stops arc blue and white.

The DASH goes in Alexandria, VA. The stops are blue and white.

The Fairfax Connector goes through parts of Fairfax County, VA—for example, to Fort Belvoir, Woodlawn, and Mt. Vernon. The stops are white, with black and yellow stripes.

The Fairfax CUE also goes through parts of Fairfax County—for example, to Vienna, George Mason, and Reston. The stops are green and gold.

Taxis

 Taxi drivers should have a license with a photo ID in a place where you can see it.

You can get a cab:

- on the street. Look for a cab with the roof light on and wave your hand.
- at your home. You can call a cab 1-2 days before you go. Usually, you can get a taxi in about 15-20 minutes, but you cannot be sure; on rainy days or Fridays, you may wait longer. Calling for a cab does not cost extra.

The District is divided into five taxi zones; each zone is divided into subzones. Your fare depends on:

- the number of zones and subzones you pass through.

- the time of day—peak or non-peak hours.
- the number of people in the cab—$1.25 more for each extra person.

The average fare is about $1.70 a mile; the most two people pay to get through the city is less than $15.

Virginia and Maryland taxis have meters. The rates are set by the county. You may pay:

- $1.40-$2.60 for the first mile.
- $1.20-$1.40 for each extra mile.
- $1 for each extra person.

Tipping. Give the driver 10%-15% of the fare.

Limousines

Limousines ("limos") usually cost about $35-$45 an hour, plus a 15% tip. Some offices use one limo service. Most limos take credit cards, cash, or checks. If your employer is paying for the limo, the tip is included in the fee.

Licensing. All limousines must be licensed. Look for:

- a B or a P at the end of the number on the license plate (in Maryland).
- a sticker on the windshield (in the District).
- a blue sticker on the bumper (in Virginia).

Information

The Metro system

General Information: 202/637-7000

- Metro police: 202/637-1245
- Lost and found: 202/962-1195

Hours of operation

Metrorail.

Monday-Friday, 5:30 am-12 midnight; Saturdays and Sundays, 8 am-12 midnight.

Metrobus.

Monday-Friday, 4 am-2 am. Individual bus schedules vary. For schedule information, call 202/637-7000

Metrorail Sales Offices.

- 12th & F St., NW entrance (underground), Washington, DC; red, blue, and orange lines; Monday-Friday, 8 am-6 pm; Saturday, 9 am-5 pm.
- Metro Headquarters, Jackson Graham Building, 600 5th St., NW, Washington, DC. 202/637-7000; Monday-Friday, 8 am-4 pm.
- The Pentagon (concourse level), Arlington, VA (blue and yellow lines); Monday-Friday, 7:30 am-3 pm.

Suburban buses

Ride-on: 301/217-RIDE

DASH: 703/370-DASH

Fairfax Connector: 703/339-7200

Fairfax CUE: 703/385-7859

Taxis

If you have a complaint or if you left something in the cab.

DC: 202/767-8370

MD

- Montgomery County: 301/217-2184
- Prince George's County: 301/925-6015

VA

- Arlington County: 703/358-4258
- Fairfax County: 703/222-8435

Words to Know

EXITFARE machine: a machine for adding more money to your subway ticket

Fare: the cost of the subway or bus

Farecard: a ticket for the Metrorail

Flashpass: a special farecard that lets you use the Metro system at a discount

ID: identification; a photo or paper that shows who you are

Kiss & Ride: places near the Metrorail stations for picking up people or dropping them off

Licensed: allowed by the city or county government to drive a taxi

Limousine: a large car, also called a "limo." You can rent a limo with a driver to get to the airport or take a group of people somewhere.

Lines: the different routes, or paths, for buses and for the subway

Lost and found: the place that has things people have lost

Meter: a machine in the taxi that tells the cost of the ride

Metrobus: the bus run by Metro

Metrorail: the subway. Metrorail connects DC, Maryland, and Virginia.

Metro system: the buses and subways that connect Maryland and Virginia to DC

Pass: a farecard, or ticket, that lets you ride on the bus or subway

Peak hours: weekdays, between 5:30 am and 9:30 am, and between 3 pm and 7 pm. All other hours are non-peak.

Subzone: a section, or part, of a zone

Token: a coin that lets you ride on the Metrobus

Transfer: a piece of paper that lets you go from bus to bus or from the subway to bus

Zone: a section, or part, of the city

How to manage your money anytime, anywhere, any way you choose.

Wherever, whenever, however you want, you can. From any phone, any Citicard Banking Center® location

TRANSFER MONEY BETWEEN ACCOUNTS OVER THE PHONE or Citibank branch. With CitiPhone Banking,℠ you can

do almost all your banking from any phone, anytime, day or night.

And together with your Citicard,® you can use our Citicard Banking Centers for full-service banking – to get cash, make deposits, pay some bills – 24 hours a day.

Of course, you can manage *all* your money at *any* Citibank branch in Washington, D.C. or Maryland.

With helpful, personalized service at every one.

Plus, our World Wallet service offers you foreign currency and travelers checks. And with our International Cheques, you can have checks issued in over 40 currencies.

To find out more, call CitiPhone Banking at **(202) 857-6700** (or **1-800-926-1067** outside the D.C. Metro area).

THE **CITI** NEVER SLEEPS®

__Money Matters__

Your Bank Check

Joe Sanchez
Marie Sanchez
701 Montgomery Place
Bethesda, MD 20814

3/5   19 93

0001

PAY TO THE
ORDER OF   *International Center* $ 42.76

Forty-two dollars and 76/100   DOLLARS

Washington Bank
1 Pleasant Street
Washington, D.C. 20005

FOR   *tapes*   *Joe Sanchez*

0000000   9987654321

Your Check Register

Check No.	Date	Payee	Payment	Deposit	Balance
0001	3/5	Int'l Ctr	$42.76		$ 96.12
	3/6	Transfer		$200	$296.12
0002	3/6	Giant	$31.19		$264.93

Banking

Why you need a bank account

If you are going to stay for more than 1 or 2 months, you need a checking account. You can use your account to pay:

- monthly bills. For example, you will pay for the phone, gas and electricity, cable TV, and rent.
- grocery bills. Most supermarkets give you a card for cashing checks (see chapter on "Food Shopping").
- day-to-day expenses. Often, you can pay for new clothes, dry cleaning, and books with a check.

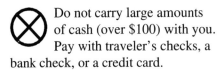 Do not carry large amounts of cash (over $100) with you. Pay with traveler's checks, a bank check, or a credit card.

Kinds of institutions

The U.S. has three main kinds of banking institutions:

- banks.
- savings and loans (S&Ls).
- credit unions.

All three have the same basic services. Banks and S&Ls are private corporations, but credit unions are owned by the members themselves. Usually, you can get a loan or a credit card more easily from a credit union than from a bank.

You may join a credit union only if you are a part of a group that has one. Many large institutions have credit unions for their employees—for example, the National Institutes of Health and the World Bank.

Choosing a bank

Services. Be sure that your branch can do the transactions you want. For example, if you will be transferring money to your home country, make sure your branch can do international transactions easily.

Federally insured (FDIC, FSLIC, or CUIC). If the institution fails, the U.S. government will give you up to $100,000 of your money back. Most banking institutions are federally insured.

Convenience. Make sure you can do transactions easily—with an ATM or by telephone. If you need to visit the bank often, it should be close to where you live or work.

The U.S. has more banking institutions than most other countries. Most banks operate in only one state or one area of the country, but you probably can get money from a bank in any area of the U.S. with your ATM card (see "Using the ATM").

Comparing banks

Many people simply use the most convenient bank, but you may want to compare:

- interest rates. All banks pay interest for savings accounts. Some pay interest for checking accounts, too.
- cost of services. Many banks charge fees for services such as using the ATM of another bank. Find out what fees you will pay and how much they cost.
- overdraft protection. If you have overdraft protection, the bank will "honor," or pay for, a check when you overdraw your account. Without overdraft protection, your check will "bounce"; you will pay a fee—sometimes as high as $25.
- the minimum balance. The minimum balance is the least amount of money you must keep in the account. If you have less, you will pay extra fees.

To open an account, you will need money to deposit. Most banks require that you always have about $100 for each account.

You will also need:

- proof of your name and address. Use
  - a letter or bill sent to your home or office address.
  - a work or student ID card.

- your Social Security card (or social insurance numbers) if you have one.
- your visa and passport.
- your employer's name and address or your student ID.
- a driver's license or other photo ID if you have one.

 Most banks are open until 2-3 pm and at least one night a week. To do everyday transactions, you can use the automatic teller machine (ATM) or the drive-in window (see "Using the ATM"). The best time to open an account is Monday-Thursday mornings. It should take 30-60 minutes.

How to open an account.

1. **Ask for the "new accounts" person at the bank.**

You will decide:

- which accounts to use. You will probably open both a savings and a checking account.
- whether each account will be single (for one person) or joint (for more than one person).

If you have more than $100,000, ask how it can all be federally insured.

2. **Fill out a form for each account.**

3. **Make a deposit.**

4. **Choose your checks.**

Decide what will be printed on your checks (name, address, phone number). You will get temporary checks to use until the printed ones come in the mail (about 7-10 days).

5. **Get a personal identification number (PIN).**

This is the code for using the ATM (see "Using the ATM").

Using your checkbook

Check register. Record every deposit and withdrawal into the check register.

Bank statement. At the end of each month, you will get a statement listing:

- all your transactions.
- the interest earned.
- the service charges.
- a beginning and ending balance.

Check this information against your register and make any corrections.

Check clearance. When you deposit a check, you may be able to use $100 of the money right away. The rest of the money has to clear. By law, banks

must "clear," or make available for use:

- a local check in 2 days.
- an out-of-state check in 5 days.
- an out-of-state check for over $5,000 in 9 days.

Checks from other countries may take as long as 3 weeks to clear.

Using the ATM

The ATM is convenient because it lets you make transactions:

- at any time or on any day.
- at another bank's machine with the same network.

To use an ATM, you will need a card and a PIN. You will make up your PIN, or code, when you open your account. The card comes in the mail about a week later.

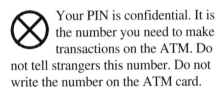 Your PIN is confidential. It is the number you need to make transactions on the ATM. Do not tell strangers this number. Do not write the number on the ATM card.

Be sure to take both your card and your receipt when you are finished. If you leave your card in an ATM, call the bank as soon as possible.

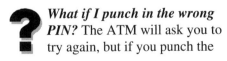 *What if I lose my card?* Call the bank right away so no one else can use it. You will get a new card.

What if I punch in the wrong PIN? The ATM will ask you to try again, but if you punch the wrong number three times, the ATM may keep your card. Call the bank to get your card back.

Credit Cards

Credit history is proof that you pay your bills on time. Unfortunately, payments you made in your home country do not get reported here. To get credit history, try to get a card or a loan—even if you do not need it.

You can get a credit card from a credit union in 2-3 weeks. If your have a foreign American Express or Diner's Club card, you can get an American one in about 2 weeks. For any other card, you may wait 4-6 weeks for approval.

The advantages of a credit card

Most Americans use credit cards to pay for bills over $10-$15. The two main advantages are:

- Paying with a credit card is simple and quick. Most merchants accept a major credit card with no questions asked.
- At the end of the month, you get one bill for all your purchases from the bank or credit card company.

The disadvantages are:

- You can buy too much—and then not be able to pay.

- If you pay only part of the amount owed, you will have high interest charges.

If I have a credit card from home, why do I need an American one? The two disadvantages of a foreign credit card are:

- The bill for a foreign card goes to your bank at home and is converted to the non-American currency—at a cost to you.
- You must keep a bank account in your home country to pay the bills.

Where to apply

Your credit union or employer's preferred bank. If you belong to a credit union, your application probably will be approved. Most embassies and many businesses can get cards for their employees from a preferred bank.

The bank or S&L where you have an account. Ask about a credit card. If possible, bring a letter from your employer stating your position, salary, and income, but do not be surprised if you do not get the card.

Banks that offer secured cards. A few banks give secured credit cards to people with no credit history. With a secured credit card, you deposit money in an account; then you can charge up to that amount with your card. This is probably the quickest way to get credit history.

41

? **What if I lose my card?** Call the card company right away—even at night or on the weekends. The toll-free 1-800 number is on your monthly bill.

Getting a Loan

Loans can be even harder to get than credit cards. Again, the best place to get a loan is at the credit union or your employer's preferred bank. When you buy an expensive item, such as a car, the dealer may be able to get you a loan; compare the terms with those of other institutions.

You will wait 3-14 business days (1-3 weeks) for a loan approval.

Some Americans borrow from finance companies. A finance company is set up mainly to lend money. Be sure the company is reliable. Check the interest rates.

Kinds of loans

Installment loans. This loan is usually for expenses such as buying a car, paying for college, or fixing up your home; most often, you must pay back the loan within 2-5 years.

Mortgage. This loan is for buying a home. Usually, you have 15-30 years to pay it back.

What to look for

Down payment. The required amount is often 10%-30%; you can put down more if you want to.

Monthly payments. The monthly payment depends on:

- the interest rate.
- the amount of the loan, or principal.
- the time period of the loan.

Interest. Rates vary. Adjustable rates are usually less than fixed rates.

Time period. The time period is the number of months or years you have to pay back the loan.

Prepayment option. This option lets you pay back the loan ahead of time.

 You will need a Social Security card or a W-8 form (certificate of foreign status). You can get a W-8 form at any bank. The W-8 form is for:

- diplomats or their family members.
- full-time employees of an international institution or family members.
- teachers or students with a J visa.

These documents may also be useful:

- **Financial reports.** Bring a financial report from your home country (see chapter on "What to Bring"). Some lending institutions will consider this; others will not.
- **Letter of recommendation.** Get a letter from your employer stating:
    – your salary.
    – your position.

- the time you are expected to stay.
- your visa type.
- **Co-signature.** You may not need a co-signature if you are borrowing from a credit union or preferred bank or if you have credit history. If you do need a co-signature, the lending institution will have a form for your co-signer or guarantor stating that he or she will pay your loan if you do not.

International Transactions

What to look for

Go to a bank that can do international transactions or to a financial service.

To compare costs, say what the transaction is and how much money is involved. Ask:

- if the bank can do the transaction for you.
- how long the transaction takes.
- whether the bank service has pick-up and delivery.

 To compare the costs, check the fees for the transaction (see below) and the rate of exchange.

Compare costs at the same time of day—preferably early morning, when European markets are open and trading.

Wiring money to the U.S.

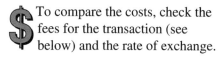 You will need the names and addresses of the foreign bank and of your U.S. bank's main branch. If possible, you should also have the routing number, or electronic address, of each bank.

You will also need:

- your account number.
- identification (any one of the following—driver's license, passport, student card, or credit card).

The transaction takes 2-3 days for developed countries, longer for countries that do not have many international transactions.

 The cost varies from $15-$30.

Wiring money from the U.S.

In addition to the information above (see "Wiring money to the U.S."), you will need:

- the account number of the bank you are wiring to and the name on the account.
- the date you want the currency to be exchanged.
- a cashier's check (this is not necessary for all transactions).

The cost is $10-$50.

Other transactions

Check conversions cost about $20-$50 a check; the cost varies according to the transaction and the individual bank. Some transactions can be done immediately; others may take as long as 3 weeks, depending on the currency and the amount of the check.

Traveler's checks (see chapters on "Before You Come" and "Traveling").

Taxes

What you will pay

You may not have to pay income or sales tax. Check with your employer and your accountant.

Income taxes. This money is with-held, or taken out of your paycheck. The amount of taxes you owe depends on your:

- taxable income, or gross income.
- deductions, or those expenses that reduce your taxable income—such as medicines, moving expenses, or foreign taxes you have paid.

Income taxes include:

- federal taxes.
- state taxes.
- local (city and/or county) tax.

Tax deadline. By midnight, April 15, you must:

- mail your tax return (a form that shows how much you owe or how much the government owes you).
- pay any taxes you owe.

So many Americans leave their taxes for the last minute that the post office is open until midnight on April 15. If you cannot pay your taxes by then, you may be able to get a 4-month extension; ask your accountant.

Sales taxes. You pay these taxes when you buy taxable items (see the chapter on "Shops & Malls").

Accountants

American tax laws are complicated —especially for newcomers. Get professional help—for example, from a certified public accountant (CPA). The accountant will:

- tell you where to send your check.
- calculate how much you owe.
- help you fill out the forms.

Often, CPAs save you more money than they charge, because they know how to apply the rules.

 Go for your first visit to a CPA as soon as you can. Sometimes, tax planning ahead of time can save money. Do not wait past December; in late March or early April, the CPA may charge more or may be too busy to accept you as a client.

The CPA will give you a better estimate of your tax situation if you bring a list of all:

- sources of income—both U.S. and foreign.
- your expenses.
- receipts for all expenses that may be deducted.
- days in and out of the U.S.

What to look for. Look for an accountant who is:

- experienced in international taxes.

- a certified public accountant.
- a member of a professional association, such as the American Institute of Certified Public Accountants.

 Accountants usually charge $85-$150 an hour. Often, the first visit is free.

45

Words to Know

Accountant: a licensed professional who helps you with your tax forms

Automatic teller machine (ATM): a money machine for transactions such as depositing and withdrawing money

Balance: the amount of money left in the account

Bounced check: a check you cannot cash because there is not enough money in the account

Cashier's check: a check made out by the bank

Certified public accountant (CPA): an accountant who meets professional standards

Checking account: a place where you keep money

Credit: the amount of money that you deposit or pay into an account; the amount of money you can borrow

Credit card: a plastic card used to buy things; you get the bill later

Credit union: a type of banking institution. You can join only if you belong to a certain group, such as a group of employees.

Deductions: expenses that reduce taxable income

Deposit: to place money in an account; the money placed in an account

Federally insured: (deposits that are) guaranteed by the federal government

Gross income: the amount of money you earn, both in and out of the U.S.

Interest: money the bank pays you for keeping money in its account(s); money you pay for borrowing

Interest rate: a percentage paid for the use of money

Network (ATM): a system of connected ATMs

Overdraft protection: a way of making sure all the checks you write are cashed—even when you don't have enough money in the account

Overdraw: to write checks for more money than is in the account

Personal identification number (PIN): the number, or code, for using the ATM

Sales tax: taxes you pay when you buy something

Savings account: an account in which to keep money you are saving

Savings and loan (S&L): a banking institution

Service charge: money paid to a bank for a specific job, such as cashing a check

Taxable income: the amount of your income you pay taxes on; gross income minus deductions

Tax return: a form that shows how much you owe the government or how much the government owes you

Transaction: an exchange of money; a deposit, withdrawal, or transfer

Transfer: to move money from one account to another

Wire (money): to send money through electronic transfer from one account to another

Withholding tax: tax money sent to the government. This tax is taken from your paycheck.

48

__Oven Temperatures__

Heat	Fahrenheit	Centigrade	British
Very low	100-250°	40-120°	Regulo 1-5
Low	300°	150°	Regulo 6
Moderate	325-350°	165-180°	Regulo 6-7
Hot	400°	205°	Regulo 8
Very hot	450-500°	235-260°	Regulo 9-10

Please note: Recipes that specify that food is to be cooked in an oven at a certain temperature assume that the oven has been *preheated* to the indicated temperature *before* the food is placed in the oven.

Allow about 15 minutes for the oven to reach the correct temperature before placing food inside. If your oven does not have a temperature control, you may purchase an oven thermometer, which will determine its temperature accurately.

Also available are *meat thermometers,* which tell the internal temperature of the meat being roasted and indicate when it is ready to be served.

__Food Shopping__

Brand name

Average amount
used at one time

Pepe's Hot and Spicy Picante Salsa

**No Additives or Fillers, No Sugar Added, No Artificial Flavors,
No Preservatives and No Oil.**

Serving size.. 2 Tbsp.
Servings per jar... 12
Sodium per serving... 60 mg.
Calories per serving.. 25

Ingredients:
**Diced Tomatoes, Onions, Peppers, Apple Cider Vinegar,
Cilantro, Garlic, Herbs and Spices.
Refrigerate After Opening.**

Net Wt. 15 1/2 oz. (439 g.)

Foods used

How much
the food weighs

The Supermarket

 If you have the time, visit a few stores before you need to buy anything.

Most supermarkets are open 7 days a week. On Monday-Saturday, they are usually open from 6 am-11 pm; on Sundays, they close in the early evening. The hours should be posted on the door.

Most grocery stores close early or all day on Thanksgiving, Christmas, New Year's Day, and other major holidays.

How to shop

1. **Bring a push cart inside the store.**

Some stores have carts with seats for children. If you are buying only a few items, walk inside and take a small basket to carry around.

2. **Find what you need.**

The aisles, or rows, have numbers at the top. Under the numbers are the names of the items in that aisle. Also, your shopping cart may have a small chart under the handle with these numbers on it.

3. **Get your check approved.**

Go to the manager's office or a desk near the entrance. The manager will sign your check. Fill out an application for a courtesy card (see "Special Services").

4. **Go to the checkout counter.**

If you are buying only a few items, look for the "express lane."

5. **The checkout worker scans each item.**

As he or she scans the items, the price comes up on a screen above the cash register. You may also check the prices on the sales slip.

6. **Give the checkout worker your coupons.**

The checkout worker will subtract the value of the coupons from your total price.

7. **Pay the cashier.**

Many major supermarkets accept cash, checks, ATM cards, debit cards, and credit cards.

8. **Leave your cart near the door.**

You can leave your bags in the cart and drive back to pick them up. If a worker helps you with your packages, you may tip him or her 50¢ a package, if you want to.

? *What if I don't have enough money at the register?* If you have a bank card, look for an ATM or ask the checkout worker if you can use your ATM card at the register. Otherwise, say, "This costs too much. I have to return some items."

What if I want to return something the next day? The large supermarkets let you return any item if it is spoiled or if you have changed your mind, as long as you return only one or two items once in a while. Take the item and the sales slip to the manager.

What if I change my mind about an item before it is paid for? Take the item off the moving belt before the cashier has scanned it. Give it to the cashier and say, "I changed my mind. I don't want this."

What you can find

Produce. Most fresh fruits and vegetables are sold by the pound. They may come packaged or loose.

At the checkout counter, the worker weighs and prices the food. The weight of the bag or other package is deducted automatically.

Meat. The meat counter has:

- fresh or frozen meat.
- chicken, turkey, and other poultry.

Meats are usually graded.

- Prime meat is the best quality and the most expensive. It has more fat and is more tender.
- Choice meat is the most common grade. It has less fat and is less tender.

- Lean meat is trimmed of fat. It can be tougher than other cuts, but most major supermarkets tenderize the meat.
- Ungraded meats can still be good, but they are usually cheaper and less tender.

To get help, ring the bell near the butcher's window. You can ask the butcher for a special cut of meat or for a package weighing exactly as much as you want (see "Special Services").

Poultry. Chicken, hens, turkey, and other poultry are usually graded AA or A. The most expensive is AA. It has less fat and is the freshest and most tender.

Seafood. The seafood counter has both fresh, frozen, and "previously frozen" seafood. Some common kinds of fish are salmon, swordfish, flounder, halibut, catfish, and tuna. Common kinds of shellfish are shrimp, clams, mussels, and oysters.

Dairy products. The dairy case is mostly refrigerated and includes eggs, milk, cheese, yogurt, and fruit juices. You can also find pickles, sauces, dips, and fresh pasta here.

Butter comes by the pound or the stick (¼ lb.). Eggs come in cartons of six (½ dozen) or twelve (1 dozen). The price depends on the size and the grade. The grades are:

- A: freshest.
- B: less fresh, but still guaranteed to be good.

Most dairy products have dates on them. The dates give the last day when the product can be sold, but the product can still be used up to a week later.

Delicatessen. The deli counter has fresh salads, hot barbecued chicken, appetizers, and other kinds of pre-pared or cooked foods. Order about ¼ pound (lb.) of meat or salad per person. When the employee weighs the food, you can see both the weight and the price in numbers above the scale.

It is not impolite to ask the employee to show you food; if you like, you can ask him or her to "add a few slices" or "take away a few spoonfuls." Ask for "a taste" if you like.

Bakery. Baked goods are usually made every day. Sometimes you can buy "day-old" breads or pastries for half-price.

You may need to take a number at the bakery or delicatessen counter. The number tells you when it is your turn to be waited on. The employee will call the numbers in order. When your number is called, step up to the counter and show your number.

Frozen foods. These include frozen vegetables, juices, ice cream, meats, fish, breads, and desserts. Frozen prepared meals, such as lasagna, burritos, or TV dinners.

Special diet foods. You can find foods with no salt or sugar. "Lite" foods have less fat or sugar.

Baby items. These include strained foods, baby cereal mixes, infant formulas, and even diapers.

Ethnic foods. You can find foods from other countries or cultures—including Oriental, Italian, Hispanic, and kosher canned goods.

Baking goods. These include ingredients for baking or cooking—such as sugar, flour, and spices. You can also find "mixes" for breads, cakes, cookies, and puddings.

Salad bar. You choose hot and cold foods and pay by the pound. The prices are posted for such items as:

- the hot salad bar, with cooked meats, chicken, pasta, soups, and chili.
- the cold salad bar, with mostly fresh vegetables and fruits; sometimes it has tuna or egg salad.
- the frozen yogurt machine; the yogurt often comes in two different flavors every day.

Take as much food as you want. The cashier at the counter weighs and prices

Check the date on the package. This tells the last day on which the product can be sold, but you can use it for a few days afterward.

the food; the weight of the container or cup is deducted automatically.

Pharmacy. This section has over-the-counter and prescription medicines (see chapter on "Medical Care"). You can also find products such as tooth-brushes, sanitary napkins, sunglasses, combs and brushes, and shaving lotion.

Photo center. You can buy film or have color photos developed here.

Figuring the Price

Labels. Look for the store's own label. These often cost less and are just as good as the food with more famous labels that are sold in many different stores.

Item price. The item price is the price of the package. If two boxes have the same amount of food, you can calculate quickly which brand is cheaper. If not, check the unit price.

Unit price. If two products are the same size, the unit price helps you calculate which product is cheaper. For example, a unit price may show the price per ounce. You can use it to compare two cans of soup—one large and one small.

Coupons. Cut these out of the "Food" section of the newspaper or out of magazines or advertising papers that come in the mail. Coupons give you a discount on a specific item. Often, the coupons cannot be used:

- after the expiration date, which is printed on the coupon.
- in all stores. For example, they may be good only in the store where you got the coupon.

Sometimes a store has "double" and "triple" coupons (two or three times the value of the coupon). For example, if you have a coupon for 25¢ off Kleenex tissues and it is a double coupon, you will get a 50¢ discount.

Sales tax. Items that are taxed have a "T" after them on the sales slip. In general, basic foods such as meat, milk, bread, and produce are not taxed. Snack foods and some house-hold items are taxed (see chapter on "Shops & Malls" for the amount of sales tax in your area).

Special Services

Special orders. Most stores take advance orders for meat, fish, or pastries. For example, you can order a turkey or ham about a week before Thanksgiving or Christmas. If you are having guests, you can order special cuts of meat, deli platters, or desserts.

Large supermarkets usually have rest rooms at the back of the store. Ask an employee where they are.

Repackaging. If you want a smaller slice of watermelon, only half of the ground meat, or a smaller piece of fish, ask. Most grocery stores are glad to repackage the food.

Special requests. If you do not see a particular kind of food you like, ask if the store can get it for you.

Coffee. Many grocery stores grind fresh coffee beans for you to take home. Some have coffee grinders next to the coffee beans so you can grind the coffee yourself.

Home delivery. Some stores offer home delivery. You can give your order over the telephone and have the groceries delivered to your house on the same day. You may have to pay for this service.

Check cashing. The courtesy or check-cashing card lets you cash a check easily. The card is good at all stores with the same name.

The large supermarkets also let you write a check for $20–$50 more than the amount of the bill. For example, if you buy $25 worth of groceries, you may write a check for $25 and get no change, or for $40 and get $15 in change.

To get a courtesy card, go to the manager's office and ask for an application. If you have a bank account in the area, you should get a card in the mail within a few weeks. Some stores give temporary cards.

Words To Know

Brand name: the name of the company on the label

Checkout counter: where you go to pay for items

Choice: the most common grade of meat

Coupon: a piece of paper that gives a discount on the price of a specific item

Courtesy or check-cashing card: a card that lets you pay with a check

Dairy products: products made from milk—such as milk, cheese, or yogurt

Debit card: a bank card used to pay for something. The money is taken out of your account right away.

Deli platter: a large plate with meats and cheeses, and sometimes with salads

Express lane: "fast lane"; lane for shoppers who have only a few items

Graded: a way of telling how good a product is. For example, meat is graded prime, choice, or lean.

Home delivery: a service that sends the groceries to your home

Item price: what something costs

Lean: a type of meat with very little fat

Packaged: wrapped up; put in a box, with paper or plastic wrap on top

Prime: the best and most expensive cut of meat

Produce: fresh fruit and vegetables

Repackaging: to pack again; putting less or more food in a package

Sales slip: a paper that lists what you bought and how much it costs

Sales tax: the value-added tax. Meat, milk, bread, and produce are not taxed. Snack foods, such as potato chips, are taxed.

Scan: to put an item in a certain place so the machine can read the price

Special order: an order for meat, fish, or pastry that the store will make for you—for example, platters or fresh whole poultry

TV dinner: a frozen meal that comes in a tray

Unit price: the price for each unit of measure—usually pounds or ounces

Ungraded: a cheaper and less tender type of meat

__Shops & Malls__

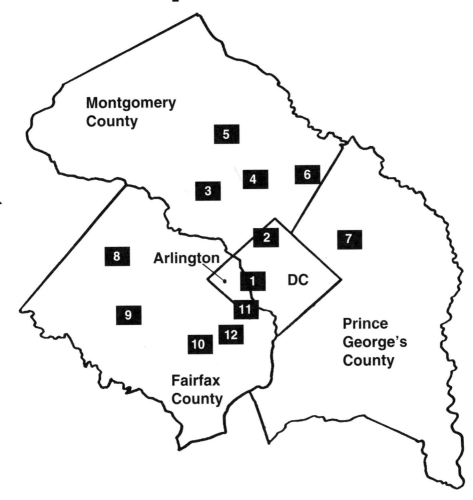

1. **Georgetown Park,** *Georgetown, DC*
2. **Mazza Gallerie,** *Friendship Heights*
3. **Montgomery Mall,** *Bethesda*
4. **White Flint,** *Rockville*
5. **Lake Forest Mall,** *Gaithersburg*
6. **Wheaton Plaza,** *Wheaton*

7. **Landover Mall,** *Landover*
8. **Tyson's Corner,** *McLean*
9. **Fair Oaks Mall,** *Fairfax*
10. **Springfield Mall,** *Springfield*
11. **Fashion Centre,** *Pentagon City*
12. **Landmark Center,** *Alexandria*

Overview

Comparing

Americans are used to "shopping around"; that is, they compare before they buy. Many internationals are surprised by the big difference in:

- the prices of the items.
- the quality of the items, or how good they are.
- the services different stores offer.

When you are "shopping around," it is not impolite to talk about the item for a while and then say you want to think about it.

Paying

How to pay. Most stores expect you to pay with a check or credit card; Americans pay with cash only if the bill is less than $30 or $40. To pay with a check, you usually need two forms of identification (ID):

- a photo ID—such as a driver's license or employee ID.
- a credit card.

Adding up the cost. Add sales tax to any item you buy. This tax is a percentage of the price.

- DC: 6%.
- MD: 5%.
- VA: 4.5%.

 Be careful when paying with a credit card. Anyone who knows the information on your card can call a mail-order company and charge an order to you. If you get a carbon paper (black paper) in between the copies of the receipt, tear it up.

Returning and exchanging

Sales slips. Always save sales slips. Most department stores will return your money if you are unhappy with a product. Some require that you return it within 2 weeks.

Many small stores offer "store credit only" for returns. That means you can get something else in the store for the same price, but you will not get your money back.

Returning items. Ask to see the salesperson or the manager of the company. If possible, have the product and the sales slip with you. Explain what you bought and when you bought it.

When you walk into a store, a salesperson may ask if you need help. Remember: you don't have to buy something just because the salesperson helps you. To look around by yourself, say, "I'm just looking, thank you." (See "Clothes Sizes" chart at the end of this chapter.)

What if I buy something that is not good and the management will not refund my money? Contact the Office of Consumer Affairs (see "Information") *in the city or county where the purchase was made.* It will tell you what to do.

Where to Shop

Shopping malls

Around Christmas time, most malls are open from 9 am-9 pm. During the rest of the year, the hours usually are:

- during the week, 10 am-9:30 pm.
- Saturdays, 10 am-5 or 6 pm.
- Sundays, 12 pm-5 or 6 pm.

Kinds of stores.

- Specialty stores. Most malls have stores specializing in books, electronics, furs, shoes, gifts, clothing, toys, jewelry, sporting goods—and anything else you can name!
- Department stores have many kinds of items. You can buy linens, jewelry, shoes, pajamas, TVs, and stationery—all in one store. Many department stores even have beauty salons and photography services. Explore!

Parking. When you park, remember:

- the number, or letter, on the post nearest your car.

- the garage level you parked on.
- which door you used to enter the mall.

Directories. The store directory is usually where main hallways come together. You may also ask at the information desk.

Rest rooms. Every mall has at least one public rest room on each floor, especially near the food court. Department stores also have rest rooms.

Restaurants.

- Food courts are large areas with tables and many types of foods. The food is served "over-the-counter," or cafeteria style. Food courts are usually less expensive than more formal restaurants. They are also good for families, because everyone can get a different kind of food.
- Formal restaurants are good for those who want a quieter meal with food brought to the table.
- Department store restaurants can be formal or informal—depending on the store.

Strip malls

Many shops are located along busy roads. Sometimes they are in separate buildings; at other times they are part of a row, or group, of stores. For example, Route 355 in Rockville, MD, and Routes 123 and 7 in Northern VA have hundreds of stores on both sides of the road.

61

Walk-ins/boutiques

A lot of areas have many little shops, larger specialty stores, and small malls. You can walk along and look at the windows, then decide where to go in. Some areas that have good "walk-in" shopping are:

- Friendship Heights, in the District (Friendship Heights Metro station on the red line).
- Georgetown, along M Street and lower Wisconsin Avenue in the District.
- Old Town Alexandria, in Virginia (King Street Metro station on the yellow or blue line).

? *What if a sales person comes to the door or calls me on the phone?* You will get many sales calls on the phone—especially around 7 or 8 pm. A few salespeople will come to your door in the middle of the day. *Remember—* it's your money! You do not have to buy anything. Just close the door or hang up the phone if you like.

Special Services

Alterations

Many stores do alterations, if necessary. Ask about the fees for this service.

Personal shoppers

Some department stores have personal shoppers. This service is free for items bought in that store. Personal shoppers can help you:

- choose gifts.
- buy clothes.
- decide what to wear for different occasions.
- choose makeup and hair styling.

Some personal shoppers even bring items to your home.

Home decorators

Like personal shoppers, home decorators give personal attention. You can use department store decorators for free. Often, they come to your home and give advice on furniture, carpets, drapes, and wallpaper. Private decorators may charge by the hour or by the amount you buy (see chapter on "Moving In").

Special orders

Sometimes, a store may not have the exact item you need. Ask the salesperson if the store can place a special order.

Shipping

Many stores will ship an item anywhere in the U.S. for a small fee. This service is convenient for sending gifts out of town.

Gifts

Gift wrapping. Usually, you can get
a free box. Many stores gift-wrap for a
fee; some stores have cards to put
inside the box.

Gift certificates. Gift certificates are
common for graduations, birthdays,
and Mother's or Father's Day. For
example, a person who has a $50 gift
certificate can spend $50 in that store.
You can buy gift certificates at many
kinds of stores—such as department
stores, record stores, and small
specialty shops.

Bridal registry. Brides often register
at a store to help people choose gifts.
The bride and groom make a list of
the items they want and give the list
to a store. When you go to the store,
the salesperson looks up the name of
the couple and shows you the items
on their list. The store also keeps track
of what has been bought already.

If you have a credit card, you can use
the phone to buy and send the gift.
You may choose the gift, charge it,
and have it mailed—without ever
leaving your house!

Baby registry. The baby registry is
like the bridal registry (see "Bridal
registry"). Ask for the children's
department.

Corporate gifts. If you need to buy
gifts for many people at work, you
can get help from a few stores. A
specialist can make suggestions and
help you decide what to buy.

Catalogs

Advantages

Catalogs allow shoppers to buy items
from their home.

You can get catalogs in:

- large department stores.
- the mail. Often catalogs come in
  the mail even if you have not
  asked for them.

Catalog shopping has two main
advantages:

- wide choice. You have more
  colors and sizes to choose from.
- convenience. You can call most
  catalogs from your home, 7 days
  a week, night or day.

The disadvantages are:

- cost of returns. If you return the
  item, you usually will not get
  back the delivery cost. Also, you
  will pay postage to send the
  product back.
- delivery delays. The company
  may not have what you ordered.
  Sometimes the delay is only a
  few days, but it may be a month
  or more.

How to order

To order by mail, cut the order form
from the catalog, fill it out, and mail
or fax it to the catalog company. The
company will need the number of
your credit card on the form or a

check. You may order catalog goods by phone if you have a credit card.

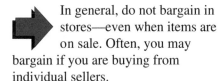 The delivery cost is usually a percentage of the cost of the item; add this to the price. You may or may not pay a sales tax—depending on the location of the store.

Bargain Hunting

In general, do not bargain in stores—even when items are on sale. Often, you may bargain if you are buying from individual sellers.

Advertisements

Classifieds. The classified ads in the back of the newspaper are mostly from people who want to sell something secondhand (used).

Store ads. Stores often advertise sale items in newspapers. If you see an item that interests you, call the store to find out more about it. Always read the fine print. Make sure you know when the sale ends and if there are any restrictions.

Special sales

When you go to a store for a sale item, take the ad with you. If the store has no more of that item, a dealer will sometimes give you a "rain check"; that means you can buy the item at the same sale price at a later time.

It is not impolite to ask the salesperson if an item will go on sale soon.

 What if I have just paid full price for an item and then see it on sale? Tell a salesperson. Show the salesperson the item and your receipt; you usually get the discount.

Discount shopping

Discount stores have lower prices. There are discount stores for almost every kind of item. Pay special attention to the return policies; sometimes there are no refunds.

Warehouse clubs are huge stores that sell name-brand products at lower prices. The prices are cheaper—sometimes almost half those in the regular stores. Usually, you can find them in suburbs such as Gaithersburg, MD, or Fairfax City, VA.

About 25% of the items in a warehouse club are food products that are frozen, canned, and boxed; most warehouse clubs do not have fresh food. Also, you may have to buy "in bulk"—for example, three detergent boxes instead of one.

Warehouse clubs also have office supplies, small appliances, sporting equipment, household products, clothes, and many other kinds of products.

To shop in a warehouse club, you usually must:

- pay a membership fee—around $25.

meet certain standards set by the club. If you work for a large company, you probably will meet these standards.

Discount stores are smaller than warehouse clubs; their prices may not be as low, but you do not have to buy in bulk or pay a membership fee. You can find discount stores for almost anything—including clothing, furniture, leather goods, shoes, and sporting equipment. Look at the ads in the newspaper to find the discount store you want.

Outlet malls get their products right from the factory and sell them for a lower price. Ask if the item is a "second," or slightly damaged; if it is, look closely to see what could be wrong. For example, look for stains or missing buttons.

Garage/yard sales are sales in private homes. Most items for sale are used. You may find antiques, old books, furniture, clothes or dishes. You cannot return what you buy, but you can bargain.

Consignment shops sell used items, such as clothing, home lamps, or books. You cannot return what you bought. Usually, you cannot bargain.

Flea markets are public markets with many kinds of items. Most flea markets are outdoors, but some larger ones are indoors.

Flea markets usually sell used items—such as furniture, clothes, jewelry, and antiques. As with yard

sales, you cannot return items, but you can bargain.

Information

Business complaints

DC

- Better Business Bureau, 1012 14th St., NW, Washington, DC 20005. 202/393-8000
- Office of Consumer & Regulatory Affairs, 614 H St., NW, Washington, DC 20001. 202/727-7103

MD

- Montgomery County Office of Consumer Affairs, 100 Maryland Ave., Rockville, MD 20850. 301/217-7373
- Prince George's County Office of Consumer Affairs, County Administration Building, Ground Floor, Upper Marlboro, MD 20772. 301/925-4700

VA

- Northern Virginia (state office), Office of Consumer Affairs, 100 N. Washington St., #412, Falls Church, VA 22046. 703/532-1613
- Alexandria Office of Consumer Affairs, P. O. Box 178 - City Hall, Alexandria, VA 22313. 703/838-4350
- Arlington County Office of Consumer Affairs, 1400 N. Courthouse Rd., Room 16,

Arlington, VA 22201. 703/358-3260
- Fairfax County Office of Consumer Affairs, Government Center, 12000 Government Pkwy., Fairfax, VA 22035. 703/222-8435

Outlet mall

Potomac Mills, 2700 Potomac Mills Circle, Woodbridge, VA 703/643-1770 (I-95 south, Woodbridge exit; follow the signs to Potomac Mills).

Words to Know

Alteration: the changing of clothes so they fit you

Baby registry: a list of gifts that parents want for their baby

Bridal registry: a list of gifts for the bride and groom

Bulk: (items) in large quantities. Usually, you get a discount for buying "in bulk."

Cafeteria: a restaurant where you serve yourself and bring the food to a table

Catalog: a book that shows pictures and tells about the items for sale. You can call or mail in your order.

Classified section: a section of the newspaper that lists items for sale

Consignment shop: a store that sells used items

Corporate gifts: gifts for people at work

Decorator: a person who helps you decide what furniture, carpets, drapes, and wallpaper to buy

Discount store: a store that sells items at lower prices

Fine print: the small writing at the bottom of an advertisement or contract. The "fine print" usually gives details—such as when you can buy the item and when you must pay.

Flea market: a public outdoor market where you can buy used furniture, clothes, jewelry, and antiques. You can bargain at a flea market.

Food court: an area in a mall or shopping center with many types of fast food restaurants

Garage/yard sale: sales in private homes. Usually items for sale are used.

Gift certificate: a kind of gift. To buy someone a gift certificate, go into the store and pay for the certificate at the cash register. When you give the certificate to your friend, he or she can use it to buy something at the store.

Gift wrap: to cover a package with pretty paper and a bow

Mall: a shopping area in one building with many kinds of stores

Outlet mall: a mall with discount stores

Personal shopper: a person who helps you choose gifts and buy clothes.

Rain check: a piece of paper that lets you buy an item for a lower price after the sale is over

Receipt: a slip of paper you get from the store when you buy something which shows the items purchased and the amount paid

Refund: to return money

Sales slip: (see "Receipt")

Secondhand: used

Specialty store: a store that sells only a few types of items—such as lamps, jewelry, or antiques

Store credit: credit you get for returning an item

Warehouse club: a big store that sells items at lower prices

Shopping

Bombay Fashions. 1085 Rockville Pike, Rockville, MD 20852. 301/424-8081. The best in Indian and Asian clothing and fabrics.

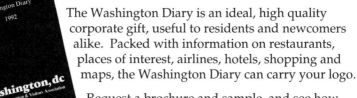

Give a gift to clients that lasts *all year long!*

The Washington Diary is an ideal, high quality corporate gift, useful to residents and newcomers alike. Packed with information on restaurants, places of interest, airlines, hotels, shopping and maps, the Washington Diary can carry your logo.

Request a brochure and sample, and see how this pocket calendar can project *your* corporate image. Inquire about other gifts with a Washington theme.

Oxford Communications
P.O. Box 10848, Alexandria, VA 22310

Tel. **(703) 922-4193** or Fax **(703) 922-7430**

"An elegant and quality product...just the image we want to project."
—J.J. Smith, Vice President, KCMS, a Kiplinger Company

Clothes Sizes

Women's clothes sizes

"Misses" Dresses, Coats & Skirts

American	3	5	7	9	11	12	13	14	15	16	18
European	36	38	38	40	40	42	42	44	44	46	48
British	8	10	11	12	13	14	15	16	17	18	20

Sweaters & Blouses

American	10	12	14	16	18	20
European	38	40	42	44	46	48
British	32	34	36	38	40	42

"Junior Miss" Dresses or Suits

American	3	5	7	9	11	13	15
European				34	36	38	40

Shoes

American	5	6	7	8	9	10
European	36	37	38	39	40	41
British	3½	4½	5½	6½	7½	8½

Men's clothes sizes

Suits, Overcoats & Sweaters

American	34	36	38	40	42	44	46	48
European	44	46	48	50	52	54	56	58
British	34	36	38	40	42	44	46	48

Shirts (Come in combination of neck and sleeve sizes [32-36])

American	14½	15	15½	16	16½	17	17½	18
European	47	38	39	41	42	43	44	45
British	14½	15	15½	16	16½	17	17½	18

Shoes

American	7	8	9	10	11	12	13
European	39½	41	42	43	44½	46	47
British	5½	6½	7½	8½	9½	10½	12½

Getting in and out of over 290 countries has never been quite this easy.

Whether you need to call another country from the U.S., or back to the U.S. from another country, no carrier gives you easier connections than Sprint.

You see, Sprint not only provides you service from the U.S. to over 290 countries and locations worldwide, we also offer low flat rates to many of those countries. And Sprint's program The Most℠ can save you even more if the person you call the most each month is in another country.

Calling the U.S. from another country can be just as easy, too, thanks to Sprint's FŌNCARD.℠ All you have to do is dial the appropriate toll-free Sprint access code to reach one of Sprint's English-speaking operators, who will bill the call to your FŌNCARD.

So, whether your goal is getting into another country or getting back to the U.S., remember that no one makes it easier than Sprint.

If only international travel were this simple. Call **1·800·829·2272**.

Sprint.

Not just another phone company.℠

___The Telephone___

Local Calls
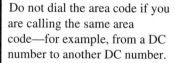
Dial:
- the area code.
- the 7-digit number.

Do not dial the area code if you are calling the same area code—for example, from a DC number to another DC number.

example:
461-4980

Long-Distance Calls

Dial:
- "1".
- the area code.
- the 7-digit number.

example:
1-912/344-0199

International Calls

Dial:
- "011".
- the country code.
- the city code.
- the 7-digit number.

example:
54-1/814-0356

Operator-Assisted Calls

Dial:
- "0" for operator assistance nationwide.
- "00" for international assistance.

An operator can help with collect calls, person-to-person calls, calling card calls, emergency calls, and general problems.

Dial "0"

Information Calls **?**
Dial:
- "411" for local information.
- "1" + the area code + "555-1212" for long-distance information.

example:1-215/555-1212

Making Phone Calls

Every number has a 3-digit area code and a 7-digit number.

For example, in the number 202/223-9000:

- "202" is the area code.
- "223-9000" is the number.

Local area codes.

- "202" for the District (DC).
- "301" or "410" for the local Maryland area.
- "703" for Northern Virginia.

Note: A number with these area codes may or may not be local from your home.

Always dial the area code for long distance calls—even if the number has the same area code as yours.

Also dial the area code if it is different from the one on the phone you are using—for example, if you are dialing from a "703" number to a "202" or a "301" number.

Some businesses have phone numbers with letters instead of numbers—for example, 202/PHONE-US. Dial the letters on the phone buttons, or the numbers that correspond to those letters.

Many businesses have "800" numbers. You can call these numbers for free—even if the office is not in the local area.

Remember: If you call a number with "976," "900," or "915," you pay extra for the call. Sometimes these numbers cost $25 an hour or more.

Finding a number

To find a telephone number:

- use the telephone book (see "Telephone Books").
- call "411" for numbers in the DC Metropolitan area (see this chapter's opener).
- call long-distance information (see this chapter's opener). Dial "0" and ask the operator for the area code if necessary.

In 1 month, from your home phone, you can make:

- 12 or fewer "411," or local information calls, for free. Each additional call is 25¢.
- three or fewer long-distance information calls for free. Each additional call is 29¢.

Calling either local or long-distance information from a pay phone is free.

Operator-assisted calls

For an extra cost, the operator can help you make a local or long-distance call. Dial "0" for calls in the U.S. or "00" for international calls.

Collect calls. The person you are calling pays for the call. To make a collect call, dial "0" + area code + number. The operator will see if the person you are calling will accept the charges, or cost, for the call.

"Person-to-person" calls. The operator first asks for the person you are calling; if the person is not there, you do not pay for the call.

? *What if I have an emergency and the number I call is busy?* Call the operator and ask for an "emergency breakthrough." The operator will ask you if this is an emergency, or a "matter of life and death." If you answer "yes," the operator will interrupt the call for you.

Local calls

$ Most local calls are free, unless you call from a pay phone (see "Pay phones" and "Ordering Phone Service").

How to dial

1. **Find out if the number is local.**

The pages in the front of the phone book list local calling areas and exchanges.

2. **Dial or press the numbers.**

- "9" if you are calling from a campus, office building, or hotel.
- the area code, if necessary.
- the 7-digit number.

3. **If you get a recorded message, leave a message on the answering machine.**

- Wait for the "beep."

- Leave your name, phone number, and a brief message.
- Hang up.

? *What if a recorded voice answers and tells me something I don't understand?* If you do not understand the recording:

- Dial "0" to speak with an operator.
- Wait; usually someone will answer the call.
- Dial "1" or any other number you hear; when someone answers the phone, explain what you need and the person will connect you to the right line.

Long-distance calls

The U.S. has four different time zones (see the opener for chapter on "Traveling"):

- Eastern: Washington, DC, time.
- Central: 1 hour earlier.
- Mountain: 2 hours earlier.
- Pacific: 3 hours earlier.

$ Several companies provide long-distance service in the U.S. The cost is different for each long-distance company. Depending on when and where you call, the cost can be about 10¢ for the first minute, or more than $60 for a 1-hour call. The three time rates are:

- 8 am-5 pm, Monday-Friday ("daytime"): most expensive.

73

- 5 pm-11 pm, Monday-Friday ("evening"): less expensive.
- 11 pm-8 am, Monday-Friday, all day Saturday, and Sunday until 5 pm ("night/weekend"): least expensive.

For example, a 1-hour call to Chicago from 8 am-5 pm costs $14, but after 6 pm it costs only $8.

Numbers with the prefix "800" are free.

Calling cards. To make a long-distance call from outside of your home, you may use a calling card; you can get one from your long-distance phone company (see "Long-distance service").

If you are using a long-distance calling card, follow the instructions on your card. If you need help, dial "0" and ask for an operator from your long-distance company.

? *What if I dial the wrong number on a long distance call?* Dial "0" and tell the operator that you got the wrong number. You will get a refund.

? *What if I have a poor connection?* Hang up and dial "0." For example, give the operator the number you dialed and say you got a poor connection. You will not have to pay for the call.

International calls

Dialing (see this chapter's opener).

$ The cost is different for each long-distance company. For example, one company charges about $1.15-$1.93 for the first minute, and $0.64-$1.08 for each additional minute for a call to Spain.

Also, the cost of the call depends on the time of day. For example, a 1-hour call to Paris from 8 am-5 pm can cost almost $65; the same call costs about $40 after 5 pm.

Pay phones

$ Local calls cost 25¢ in Maryland or Virginia and 20¢ in the District. Use exact change; extra money is not returned.

How to dial from a pay phone

1. Lift the receiver and listen for the dial tone.

2. Put your money in the slot.

If you need to call long distance, first dial the number; the operator will tell you how much you need to pay.

3. Dial the number.

4. Deposit more money if necessary.

The operator will tell you when your time is running out.

? ***What if I lose money in a pay phone?*** Dial "0" for operator. For example, say, "I put two quarters in the machine. I dialed the number, but the line was busy. When I hung up, I didn't get my money back." The operator will reconnect you for free or will mail you a refund check.

Ordering Phone Service

Local service

C&P Telephone is the only local phone company in the Washington area.

To get phone service in your home, call C&P (see chapter on "Moving In"). Decide:

- how you want to be listed in the phone book (see chapter on "Moving In").
- if you want a flat rate or per-call service (see "Regular service plans").
- which features you want. Call C&P Telephone's business office. Ask for a list of the special services it offers (see "Special Services").

Regular service plans.

- unlimited (flat rate) service. It costs about $18 a month. You can make as many local calls as you want.

- per-call (measured or message rate) service. This costs less than the flat rate service, but you may pay more if you make a lot of calls.

For example, in Prince George's County, the measured service plan costs about $9 a month for 65 calls; you pay 9¢ for each extra call. This plan is good for a person who makes only 2-3 calls per day.

Special services. A few popular services are:

- Answer Call. Takes messages when you do not answer the phone. $6.50-$10 a month.
- Call Waiting. Lets you get a second phone call when you are using the phone. You can answer the second call without hanging up on the first person. $3.50 a month.
- Call Forwarding. Lets you get your calls at another number. For example, you can forward your calls to an answering service or to your office. $3.50 a month.

Long-distance service

To make a call outside of the local calling area, order service from a long-distance phone company.

Call two or three different companies and ask about their plans (see "Information"). Compare services and prices. Find out the rates for the places you call most often. Also ask about the company's plans for international calls.

Telephone Equipment

 You can rent telephones from AT&T (see chapter on "Moving In"). You can buy phones from phone or electronic stores.

There are two kinds of phones: touch tone and dial.

Touch tone (push button). With a touch tone phone, you make a call by pressing the buttons with the numbers. Touch tone phones have three advantages:

- Pressing the buttons is faster than dialing.
- Some business calls are faster and more direct with a touch tone.
- You must have a touch tone phone to use certain features, such as Answer Call.

Rotary (pulse). With a dial phone, you make a call by dialing instead of pushing the buttons with the numbers (see "Touch tone" above).

Usually, phones cost $20-$40.

Special features

Multiple lines. You can have different telephone numbers on one phone.

Hold button. You can have a person wait on "hold" until you pick up the line again.

Redial. You can redial the last number you called or tried to call by pressing one button.

Speed dialing. You can store several numbers in the phone. When you call one of these numbers, you only have to press one button.

Speaker phone. You can hear and talk to someone on the phone through a speaker without holding the receiver. This also lets more than one person listen to a call.

Special phones

Cordless (portable) phones. The receiver has no wires; so you do not have to stay in one place while you are on the phone.

Phone/fax machine. The phone also serves as a facsimile machine.

Cellular (wireless) phone. These are especially popular for use in the car.

To get the best price, buy a service contract. The contract requires that you pay for:

- cellular phone service for a set period of time (6 months-1 year).
- an activation charge (about $40).
- calls you make and receive. These calls cost much more than regular phone calls. For example, a call that would cost 4¢ on your home phone might cost $3 from a cellular phone.

Service packages (phone plus activation) cost from $100 for a hand-held portable to over $1,500. Be sure to compare prices at several stores. The average monthly cellular phone bill is about $70.

Answering machines

Most Americans have answering machines or use the C&P Answer Call feature (see "Special services"). If you do not answer the phone, the person calling you can leave a message.

You can buy an answering machine at a department or discount store or a phone or electronic store. The cheapest machines cost about $25.

Telephone Books

When you move into your new home, you will get two C&P phone books for free:

- the yellow pages.
- the white pages.

The yellow pages

Ads and listings. C&P has two "yellow pages" books—an A-K book and a L-Z book. The main part of both books is the advertisements and listings of goods and services.

Action index (pages with red borders). Use these pages to find the types of businesses listed in the yellow pages. These pages are at the back of the L-Z book.

Other yellow pages information.

- Emergency numbers are at the beginning of the A-K book.
- Metro area information such as sports, theaters, subways, and maps is at the beginning of the A-K book.
- A list of businesses is in the white section at the beginning of each book.
- Government offices are in the blue pages of the A-K book. They are listed by government level (city, county, state, DC, and U.S. or federal) and then by the department. For example, your local post office is listed under "U.S. Government."

The white pages

Phone company information and emergency numbers are in the white pages with the black borders. For example, you can find telephone rates and kinds of services here.

Home phone numbers are listed alphabetically by the person's last name in the second section of the book.

Government offices are in the blue pages. They are listed by government level (city, county, state, DC, and U.S.) and then by department.

A list of businesses in the Metro area is in the white pages at the back of the book.

The perfect fit for calls all over the world.

In the U.S., you have a choice of international long distance companies. And it's an easy choice. Because with more savings to more places than any other long distance company, MCI is the perfect fit for you — whether you're calling in the U.S. or around the world.

To find out about how you can save on your calls to anyone, anywhere the world over, call an MCI Customer Service Representative toll-free: **1-800-444-3333.**
Or for service in the language of your choice, call toll-free:

Para ayuda en Español	**1-800-950-4652**
國語客戶服務	**1-800-444-0750**
粵語客戶服務	**1-800-777-0958**
한국어 고객서비스	**1-800-933-0550**
日本語カスタマーサービス	**1-800-888-4800**

Information

C&P: see "Information" in chapter on "Moving In"

Long-distance companies.

- Allnet: 202/429-1740
- AT&T: 1-800/222-0300
- MCI: 1-800/444-3333
- Sprint: 1-800/877-7746

Words to Know

Answer Call: an "extra" service that lets you get messages when you do not answer the phone

Area code: the 3-digit code for the region where you live—for example, "202" for Washington, DC

Call Forwarding: an "extra" service that lets you send your calls to another number

Call Waiting: an "extra" service that lets you switch to another caller while you are on the phone with someone

Cellular phone: a wireless phone— such as a car phone

Collect: a kind of long-distance call. The person you are calling pays for the call.

Cordless phone: a kind of phone. The receiver is not attached to the main part of the phone.

Country code: a number you dial to call a country. Each country has its own code.

Dial tone: the humming sound you hear when you pick up the receiver

Flat rate: a kind of basic service. The price for this service is the same every month; you can make as many local calls as you want at no extra cost.

Hold: to wait. To put someone "on hold" is to have that person wait on the phone while you talk to someone else.

Information: the number you dial to get someone's telephone number—"411" for the Washington metropolitan area

Local: in the "free" area for your phone service

Long-distance: not in the "free" area for your phone service

Measured rate: (see "Per-call service")

800 number: a free call. You can call any "800" number for free (see "Toll-free numbers").

900 number: a kind of telephone number. You pay for the call.

Per-call service: a basic phone service. You pay extra for each local call after you have made 60 calls within a month.

Person-to-person: a kind of long-distance call. You tell the operator the name of the person you want to talk to. If the person is not there, the operator does not put the call through.

Pulse phone: (see "Rotary phone")

Receiver: a part of the phone. You hold the receiver in your hand.

Rotary phone: a kind of phone. You dial the numbers to make a call

Speaker phone: a phone with which you can hear and talk to someone without holding the receiver

Speed dialing: an "extra" service. It lets you call up to 30 numbers fast.

Toll-free ("800") numbers: a free call. You can call any 800 number for free.

Touch tone phone: a kind of telephone operated by pressing buttons with numbers on them.

Unlimited rate: (see "Flat rate")

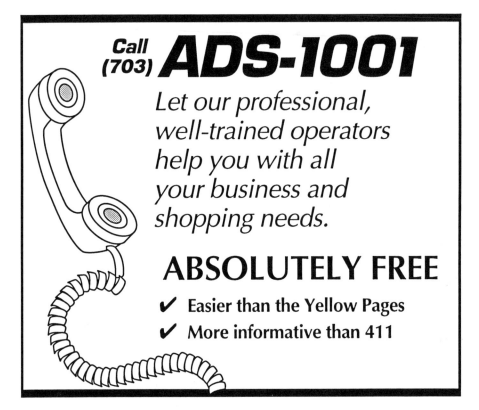

Your Mail

Return address

Air Mail stamp

Tomiko Yamada
1716 Woodmont Ave.
Bethesda, MD 20814
U.S.A.

Air Mail

Miss Akiko Yamada
7-3-6 Kyodo, Setagaya-ku
Tokyo, Japan F156

City, Country

Domestic

Tomiko Yamada
1716 Woodmont Ave.
Bethesda, MD 20814

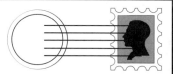

Mr. Thomas Barett
066 Berkley Ave.
Albany, CA 94706

City, State (California), Zip Code

Getting to the Post Office

Location. Every post office has a U.S. flag near it and the words "U.S. Post Office" on the building. To find the closest post office, call the postal service (see "Information").

Services. At the post office you can:

- mail letters and packages.
- buy stamps and supplies—such as envelopes and boxes.
- buy money orders.
- rent a post office box. The smallest boxes cost $19 for 6 months.

 The post office is usually open Monday-Friday from 8 or 8:30 am-5 pm and on Saturday mornings until 12 noon or 1 pm.

Domestic

 A domestic first-class letter costs 29¢ for the first ounce (oz.) and 23¢ for each additional ounce.

Ways to send

First class. The most common way to send letters and postcards. Mail usually arrives in 2-3 days, depending on the distance. A letter weighing up to one ounce costs 29¢; each additional ounce costs 23¢. Postcards cost 19¢.

Fourth class ("parcel post"). Regular mail service for packages that weigh 1 pound (lb.) or more. Packages may take up to 8 days to arrive.

Book rate. A lower rate for sending books.

Express. Overnight mail. The cost is $9.95 for an letter that weighs 8 ounces or less.

Priority. First-class mail that weighs over 11 ounces. The cost is $2.90 for up to 2 pounds; $4.65 for up to 4 pounds; and $5.45 for a 5-lb. package.

Collect-On-Delivery (COD). You pay for an item when the letter carrier delivers it to you.

 Do not mail cash; if the money gets lost, you will not be able to replace it. Use a check or money order.

Note: You can insure any package for a small fee. Ask the clerk at the post office.

To mail a letter or package in the U.S., you must write the zip code. The zip code is a 5- or 9-digit number that shows the U.S. postal area. Some zip codes in Washington, DC, are 20001, 20007, and 20016. To find the zip code for an address, call any post office or go there and use the zip code directory.

How to mail a domestic letter

1. Write the addressee's name, street address, city, state, and zip code.

2. Write your own address in the upper left-hand corner of the envelope.

If you have the wrong address, the letter carrier will return the letter.

3. Buy a stamp if you are sending the letter regular first class.

You can buy stamps at any post office or at some supermarkets. (For certified or registered letters, go to the post office.)

4. Put your letter in a *blue* mailbox.

You can find these boxes:

- on the street—especially near the post office.
- at airports.
- in shopping malls.

Note: Read the words in white on the box. Some mailboxes are only for express mail.

You can also leave your letter in the mailbox outside your door or the mail slot in the door of your house; the letter carrier will pick it up.

Mailing packages

Wrap the package. Mark the box in large letters on the front and back:

- "FRAGILE" for objects that could break.
- "DO NOT BEND" for photographs or documents.
- "DO NOT X-RAY" for computer disks and film.
- "PERISHABLE" for foods that might spoil.

Go to the post office. The clerk will weigh the box and put on the postage.

 What if a package does not get there? Ask the postal clerk to "put a trace on the package" to see if the postal system can find it.

International

Letters/packages

 An international airmail letter costs about 50¢ for the first ½ ounce and 45¢ for each additional ½ ounce. You can also buy airletters for 45¢. Airmail letters take about 7-10 days.

A 2-lb. package costs about $6.50 to send out of the country, surface (not by air) mail; it often arrives several weeks later. A 2-lb. airmail package costs about $11-$12 and takes 5-7 days.

Express

International express mail takes 2-3 days; the number of delivery days is not guaranteed. (For guaranteed overnight delivery to another country, use a private service.)

 Some countries limit package weight. Ask the postal clerk about the rules of the country to which you are sending the package.

Private Services

Mailing

Private services do some jobs that the post office does not. For example, some services:

- pick up the mail at your door.
- mail overnight to countries outside the U.S.

 You will pay a pick-up fee. Some services have letter-size mailing envelopes, but you must seal and label any boxes yourself. The cost is about $15 a day for express mail with pick-up.

International express. Sample costs are:

- An 8-oz. express package costs about $22 to send door-to-door from Washington, DC to Paris. It takes 2-3 days.
- A 1-lb. package costs about $28, a 2-lb. package about $55.
- Overnight service can cost up to $300.

Domestic. For example, a 5-lb. package sent Next-Day Air from Washington, DC to San Francisco costs about $20.

How to pay. Most private services let you pay with a credit card. If you have an account with that company, you can charge it on the phone.

Other services

Wrapping. Often, private services have more packaging and office supplies than the post office. Also, the clerk will do the wrapping for you. The boxing and wrapping can cost from 75¢-$5, depending on the size of the package.

Mailboxes. Some private services rent mailboxes for about $15-$30 a month. When you travel, the service will forward your mail to the city where you are staying; the cost is about $5 extra each time.

Telegrams ("Mailgrams"). You can use a telegram to send a message quickly here or abroad. Western Union, the only company that sends telegrams, has an 800 service number to take orders and answer questions.

A 15-word domestic telegram, including personal delivery, costs about $30. The rates for international telegrams ("wires") vary by country.

Faxing and copying. Faxes inside the U.S. cost $1-$2 per page; international faxes may cost $5-$6.

Copies can be made at printing offices, libraries, private mail services, and at a few post offices. The price ranges from 5¢-25¢ a copy.

Information

Consumer Advocate Number (for the post office closest to your home): 202/268-2284

Postal Answer Line (for general information): 202/526-3920. For example, you can find out:

- the cost of sending a first-class letter anywhere in the world.
- the cost of sending a package anywhere within the U.S.
- what to do when you are moving (see chapter on "Moving In").
- how long an express letter or package will take.

Western Union: 1-800/325-6000

Words to Know

Book rate: a lower rate for sending books

Certified mail: a type of first-class mail. You get a signed card proving that the person received the mail.

Collect-on-delivery (COD): a type of shipping from a store or catalog company. You pay for the item when you get it.

Express mail: overnight mail

First-class mail: the most common way to send letters and postcards

Fragile: an item that can break easily

Money order: a check you can buy at the post office or the bank. You can send the check in the mail.

Parcel post: regular mail service for packages that weigh 1 pound or more

Post office box: a locked box in the post office where your mail is kept until you pick it up

Priority mail: first-class mail that weighs more than 11 ounces

Registered mail: mail that is guaranteed special care and security

Surface mail: mail sent by ground or boat

Zip code: a 5- or 9-digit number that shows the U.S. postal delivery area in the United States

Mail

Parcel Plus. 3509 Connecticut Ave., NW (Cleveland Park Metro), Washington, DC 20008. 202/244-6669. Ship U.S., international. Packing boxes, faxing and copying.

Finding a New Home

Townhouse (rowhouse)

Apartment (condominium)

Detached house (colonial)

Detached house (split-level)

Illustrations reprinted with the permission of Weichert Relocation Co.

Main Areas

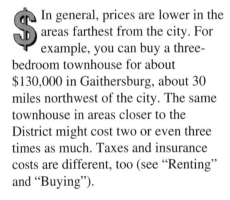 You may look for a home in the city of Washington, or the District of Columbia (known as the District, or DC). Washington, DC, is the only city in the U.S. that is not part of a state. It stands by itself because it is the nation's capital.

Next to the city are the two states of:

- Maryland. The two Maryland counties, or smaller administrative areas, closest to the District are Montgomery County and Prince George's County.
- Virginia. The two Virginia counties closest to the District are Arlington County and Fairfax County.

In general, prices are lower in the areas farthest from the city. For example, you can buy a three-bedroom townhouse for about $130,000 in Gaithersburg, about 30 miles northwest of the city. The same townhouse in areas closer to the District might cost two or even three times as much. Taxes and insurance costs are different, too (see "Renting" and "Buying").

The District

In general, homes in the District are close to museums, restaurants, and theaters. Some are particularly good for singles. Most neighborhoods are near the Metro. Check the area for safety.

The suburbs

Maryland and Virginia are the suburbs, or living areas near the city. In general, the houses are bigger, with more land and trees. Check the time it takes to get to work during rush hours.

You can find the same general types of communities in each state, but there are big differences between the individual communities. Decide what is important to you. Then find the community that has what you want.

Communities

The different types of communities are:

- rural areas. Many houses are big and far apart, with land and trees. You have a lot of space and

---

Before you rent or buy a home, look around the neighborhood after dark. Ask the neighbors if there have been any crime problems recently. You may also call the local police and ask about crime in the area (see "Information").

privacy, but you need a car to get to most places.

- suburban developments. Some suburban homes are in developments. The homes are closer together than rural homes, but many are still big, with land and trees.
- suburban cities or towns. Several suburban areas are cities or towns such as Falls Church, Alexandria, Reston, Gaithersburg, Rockville, and Bethesda. Many homes in these areas have big lots and trees, but they are closer to schools, libraries, and stores.

What to look for

Schools. Many families want areas with good schools. The public schools are run by the different counties. Find out which schools are best before you decide where to live (see chapters on "Your Young Child" and "Your Older Child").

Residents/neighbors. Are any children waiting for the school bus in the morning or playing in the yards? Do both husband and wife work? If so, would you or your spouse mind being alone all day?

Public transportation. How far is the bus or subway stop? How often do the buses run? Do they run on weekends (see chapter on "Getting Around")?

Stores and other services. Look for good restaurants, shops, beauty salons, libraries, or houses of worship—whichever are most important to you.

Distance from a major road. If you live near a major road such as routes I-95, 395, 495, 270, or 50, driving around will be much faster.

The Fair Housing Law

By law, no homeowner or landlord can refuse to rent or sell to someone because of race, sex, country of origin, or religious beliefs. Also, homeowners cannot refuse to rent or sell to families with children, but they can refuse to rent to families who:

- have pets.
- do not have enough money.
- have too many people for the size of the home.

If you think someone is disobeying this law, call the Office of Fair Housing and Equal Opportunity (see "Landlord-Tenant Relations" in "Information").

Who Can Help

 The housing office of your college or employer may give you some help. But many newcomers use a real estate agent, relocation center, or rental service.

What to look for. Pick someone who:

- is trained. Be sure the professional is a member of an association of realtors (see "Information"). To be a member, the professional must be certified.
- pays attention to what you want and what you can afford.

- knows the area. If you don't know where you want to live, you may have to use several agents or go to a relocation center.
- has patience. Do not let an agent pressure you into making a decision before you are ready.
- is experienced. How long has the agent been selling/renting homes? Does he or she work full-time or part-time?

⊗ Many internationals try to find agents who speak their own language, but also ask yourself: Would I trust this person in my own country? Is this agent experienced? Does this agent want to help me?

Types of agents. The two types of real estate agents are:

- a seller's agent. Most agents are seller's agents—that is, they work for the seller, not the buyer. For example, by law, they tell the seller your "bottom price."
- a buyer's agent. Some agents work only for the buyer, not the seller. A buyer's agent usually gets a fee from the buyer ($220 or more). You will get this money back when you buy or rent a home.

Ask if the agent will help you:

- negotiate the best deal.
- find out everything—both good and bad—about the home and the area.

Renting

In medium-priced areas, rentals range from $600 a month for a studio or efficiency (one room with kitchen and bath) to $1,300 for three-bedroom homes.

Furnished apartments and homes cost about 50% more, but you can rent furniture separately at less cost.

Many students rent:

- a basement apartment in a rowhouse; the cost is usually about $700-$1,100 a month.
- a room in a family home for about $300-$500 a month. This price does not include food; usually, you get
  - a private bedroom and bathroom.
  - the use of a washer and dryer.
  - the use of the kitchen to prepare your meals.

Usually, you pay a fee for the rental application—$25-$50. This covers the cost of the credit check.

How much you can afford

In general, do not spend more than 28%-33% of your income on monthly payments—including the rental payment, any parking and association fees, and the insurance costs. This percentage can change according to the debts you have or the taxes you owe.

When you apply for a lease, you need to show your driver's license or other photo ID. You will also need the following information:

- the name of your employer or school.
- your income for the past 2 years and how much you expect to earn this year.
- your previous address and the name of your previous landlord, if possible.
- local references, if possible (your employer, embassy, or sponsor).
- the name of your local bank.

How to rent a home

Begin your search.

Many real estate agents both sell and rent homes. Most prefer to sell rather than rent, but some housing professionals specialize in rentals.

1. Meet with the housing professional helping you.

During the meeting, the agent or broker will:

- ask what kind of home and community you want.
- ask about your salary and the amount of money you have in the bank. Then he or she will tell you how much you are "qualified," or able to pay.
- give you listings of homes that fit your needs.

2. Visit the places you have chosen.

Most agents will drive you to the homes; rental services give directions. The owner will probably not be there, but you can ask the agent or rental office questions.

3. Try to negotiate the price.

Apartments owned by a business often have a fixed price, but private owners may be willing to negotiate. Sometimes, you may get a month of free parking or a lower rental rate. The agent will tell the owner any offer you make.

4. Read the lease or have someone else read and translate it for you.

Be sure everything you expect to get is in the lease; for example, if the agent told you the rent includes parking, the lease should say so.

5. Fill out the application form and pay the application fee.

6. Sign the lease.

7. Make your first payment.

This payment includes the security (or damage) deposit—usually equal to 1 month's rent.

After you move out, the owner or manager will inspect the home. If everything is in good order, you will get your deposit back. If you have caused some damage, your deposit will pay for repairs.

⊗ Be sure you can break the lease, or leave early if you want to. Two or 3 years is a long time! If you need to "break the lease," you may have to pay—usually 1 or 2 months' rent, but maybe more. You may also have to give notice, or tell the landlord that you are leaving ahead of time. The number of weeks' or months' notice you must give should be in the lease.

The lease

The lease should include:

- how much the deposit is.
- how much rent you must pay and when you must pay it.
- what other payments you must make—such as parking; if you pay for parking, find out how many spaces you get.
- whether a washer and dryer are included.
- what will happen if you break the lease or move out early (see the warning above).
- what other rules you must follow, such as not having pets.
- what fees or costs the landlord pays—such as utilities, services, fertilizing the lawn, pest control, or repairs.

Monthly payments

Rent. This is the largest payment.

Insurance. This protects your furniture, clothes, and other possessions in case of fire or theft (see chapter on "Moving In").

Utilities. Rental payments sometimes include utility costs. The average bill for a one-bedroom apartment is about $50-$100; the average bill for a three-bedroom house can range from $75 to $250 (see chapter on "Moving In").

Parking fees. If you live in an apartment or condo, you may have parking fees—often $65 or higher.

Water and sewage. The average quarterly bill (every 3 months) for a family of four is $110.

Telephone. A basic monthly fee is charged for telephone service. The monthly fee is less than $20; extra features and long-distance calls add to the cost. If you make many international calls and talk a long time, your phone bill can be as high as $100-$200 a month (see chapters on "Moving In" and "The Telephone").

❓ *What if the landlord does not follow the terms of the lease—for example, if he does not fix a broken pipe?* If necessary, call the office of Landlord-Tenant Relations (see "Information").

Buying

How much you can afford

In general, do not spend more than 28%-33% of your salary on the monthly payments—mortgage principal, interest, property taxes, and insurance. As with rentals, this percentage can change according to the debts you have or the taxes you owe.

When buying a home, remember the closing and other fees you pay right away. These fees include the cost of a lawyer, points, homeowner's insurance, and the loan application fee. For example, closing costs for a $200,000 home are around:

- $3,400 in DC.
- $6,100 in Maryland.
- $2,200 in Virginia.

Often, the bank or the seller will agree to pay some of these costs. Negotiate.

How to buy a home

1. Find a housing professional.

This professional can give you advice as you look for and buy a home.

2. Look over listings.

The agent will show you listings of available homes. Choose the ones you want to visit.

3. Visit the homes.

The agent will drive you there.

4. Find out more.

For example, find out:

- how old the home is.
- what monthly fees the present homeowner is paying; the listing will have this information.
- what the taxes are.

- how long the builder has been in business (if the home is new).
- what comes with the house —for example, draperies or rugs.

5. Negotiate.

Usually sellers ask for more than they expect to get. Sometimes a buyer and seller make several offers and counter-offers before they agree on a price.

6. Sign a contract and give a deposit.

Both the seller and the buyer sign an agreement, but the contract should go through only if a professional home inspector finds the home in satisfactory condition (see step 8). Your deposit is part of your down payment.

7. Look for financing.

Your agent can help you find financing. You may be able to get financing from your credit union if you belong to one.

8. Have the home inspected.

The inspection should cost about $200-$250 or more, but it may save you a lot of money in the end. Be sure to choose an inspector who is a member of the American Society of Home Inspectors; all members are certified.

Inspections help you:

- find out if the home will need any major repairs—either now or in a few years. Often, the seller pays the cost of any major repairs that are needed right away.
- learn how to care for your home—for example, when to clean the furnace or how to work the appliances.

9. Apply for a mortgage.

Fill out an application (see "Renting" to find out what you will write on the application).

The mortgage process can take 2 to 3 weeks, sometimes longer, to complete.

10. Buy insurance.

You will need this insurance before your mortgage is approved (see chapter on "Moving In").

11. Find a lawyer.

You will need one to check the deed. If you like, your agent can help you find a lawyer.

12. Close the sale.

The seller, buyer, attorneys, bank representatives, and real estate brokers meet. At this time you sign the mortgage. Ask your agent ahead of time what will happen and how much it will cost. You will pay:

- the closing costs—including taxes and fees to the government.
- the rest of your down payment.
- part of your first monthly payment for the loan.

Monthly expenses

Mortgage. This is the largest payment.

Taxes. The amount you pay depends on where you live and the cost of the home. The approximate monthly property taxes for a $200,000 home are:

- DC: $160.
- Montgomery County: $205.
- Prince George's County: $235.
- Arlington County: $130.
- Fairfax County: $185.

The cost of your insurance depends on:

- the cost of your home.
- the age of your home.
- the location of your home.

Usually, your insurance and tax payments go into escrow, or into a special bank account. When the payment is due, the bank will make the payment for you from this account.

- the use of safety devices—such as a burglar alarm system.

The yearly cost of insurance for a $200,000 home (about 40 years old) is about:

- DC: $360-$730.
- MD: $340-$390.
- VA: $330-$370.

Note: The lower prices above are for homes with alarm systems; the higher prices are for homes that do not have alarm systems. Remember—these costs are not exact!

Condominium or homeowner's association fees. If you buy a town house or condominium, you will pay a monthly maintenance fee. This fee can be as high as $1,000-$2,000 a month, but it is usually lower. It may include a swimming pool, health club, and tennis courts.

See "Renting" for costs of utilities, parking, and telephone payments.

Abbreviations

Note: You will see these abbreviations in the classified ads for places to rent or buy.

Appt: Appointment

Apt: Apartment

Balc: Balcony

Bdrm: Bedroom

Bsmt: Basement

CAC: Central air conditioning

CATV: Cable television

DR: Dining room

D/W: Dishwasher

Effcy: Efficiency

Elec: Electricity

Hdwd flrs: Hardwood floors

Ht: Heat

Immed: Immediate

Incl: Included

Kit: Kitchen

Lbr: Library

Prkg avail: Parking available

Redec: Redecorated

Refs req: References requested

TH: Townhouse

Utils: Utilities

W/D: Washer and dryer

W/W: Wall-to-wall carpeting

Information

Association of Realtors

DC: 202/628-4494

MD

- Montgomery County: 301/590-2000
- Prince George's County: 350-7700

Northern VA: 703/207-3200

Landlord-Tenant relations

DC: Office of Tenant Rights: 202/737-7315

MD

- Montgomery County Office of Landlord-Tenant Relations: 301/217-3660
- Prince George's County Office of Consumer Protection: 301/528-8662

VA

- Landlord-Tenant Relations Office: 703/691-3214
- Office of Fair Housing and Equal Opportunity: 202/275-0848

The Police Crime Division

DC: 202/727-4100

MD

- Montgomery County: 301/279-8000
- Prince George's County: 301/336-8800

VA

- Arlington: 703/358-4252
- Alexandria: 703/838-4636
- Falls Church: 703/241-5054

Words to Know

Application fee: money you pay for someone to look at your application

Buyer's agent: a real estate professional who helps a buyer find a home. This agent works for the buyer, not the seller.

Closing costs: fees you pay when you sign the mortgage

Condominium (condo): one of many homes in a building. Usually, each condo is owned by the family who lives in it.

Condominium association fees: money you pay for the care of the condo building

Credit check: a check to make sure you can afford to buy a home and that you pay your bills

Credit union: a banking company owned by the workers and members of an organization

Deed: a document that shows who owns the property

Detached house: a home that is not attached to another house

Development: a group of similar houses in one area, usually made by the same builder

Down payment: money you pay when you buy a house; a deposit

Efficiency: a small apartment— usually with one main room, a kitchen, and a bathroom (see "Studio")

Escrow: money you have paid that is set aside by the bank for taxes and insurance

Financing: the way you get money to pay for a house

Homeowner's association fees: money you pay for front desk service, swimming pool, etc.

Insurance: a way to protect your belongings and property

Lease: a written agreement between a tenant and landlord

Mortgage: money a bank lends you to buy a house

Qualified: able to afford, or to pay

Real estate agent (realtor): a housing professional who can help you find a home to buy or rent

References: your employer or another person who can give the bank information about your job, income, or ability to pay

Relocation center: a place with professionals who help you find a home and learn about the area

Rentals: rooms, apartments, or houses you rent rather than buy

Rowhouses: houses that are attached to each other on the sides, usually found in the city

Rural: an area in the country (not near a city)

Security deposit: money paid to a landlord before a place can be rented. You get this money back if you do not damage the house in any way.

Seller's agent: a real estate professional who helps someone sell a house. This agent works for the seller, not the buyer.

Studio: a one-room residence with a kitchen and bath

Suburb: an area where people live near a city. In the Washington area, the suburbs are in Maryland and Virginia.

Townhouses: homes that are attached to each other at the sides, usually found in the suburbs

Utilities: electricity and gas

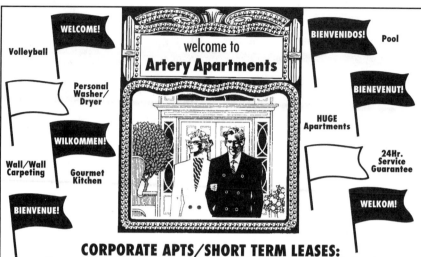

WELCOME! · Volleyball · Personal Washer/Dryer · WILKOMMEN! · Wall/Wall Carpeting · Gourmet Kitchen · BIENVENUE! · welcome to **Artery Apartments** · BIENVENIDOS! · Pool · BIENEVENUT! · HUGE Apartments · 24Hr. Service Guarantee · WELKOM!

CORPORATE APTS/SHORT TERM LEASES:

Corporate apartments are available at many locations, fully furnished and accessorized with the amenities you desire. Flexible short term leases are also available on most apartments.

24-HOUR GUARANTEED MAINTENANCE:

We respond to your maintenance concerns within 24-hours or your rent is FREE until your problem is resolved.

30-DAY LIVING GUARANTEE:

Security deposit and application fee refunded 30 days from move-in if the renter is not COMPLETELY satisfied.

COMPARE AND SEE HOW NICELY YOU'll FIT UNDER THE ARTERY ROOF.

CALL 1-800-877-RENT

for FREE, personal one-on-one relocation assistance

WE HAVE 28 COMFORTABLE, AFFORDABLE & CONVENIENT LOCATIONS

We would like to accept your offer to help us find an apartment in the WASHINGTON METROPOLITAN area and to furnish us with brochures and any additional information that will be useful when we move. The following questions are answered to help expedite the gathering of information which will be sent to us free of charge and as soon as possible.

SEND TO: ARTERY PROPERTY MANAGEMENT, INC., 7200 Wisconsin Ave., Suite 1100, Bethesda, MD 20814

Name_____ Date_____
Current Home Address_____ Phone No._____
City_____ State_____ Zip Code_____
Anticipated Date Of Arrival In Washington_____
Temporary Washington Metropolitan Address_____
City_____ Phone No._____
Company Address/Or Government Affiliation In Washington_____
Number In Family_____ Number Of Adults_____ Number Of Children_____
Ages Of Children_____ Number Of Pets_____ Kind_____

THIS COUPON WILL ALSO ENTITLE YOU TO $50.00 OFF YOUR FIRST MONTH'S RENT.

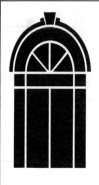

The perfect fit for calls all over the world.

In the U.S., you have a choice of international long distance companies. And it's an easy choice. Because with more savings to more places than any other long distance company, MCI is the perfect fit for you — whether you're calling in the U.S. or around the world.

To find out about how you can save on your calls to anyone, anywhere the world over, call an MCI Customer Service Representative toll-free: **1-800-444-3333.** Or for service in the language of your choice, call toll-free:

Para ayuda en Español	1-800-950-4652
國語客戶服務	1-800-444-0750
粵語客戶服務	1-800-777-0958
한국어 고객서비스	1-800-933-0550
日本語カスタマーサービス	1-800-888-4800

_____Moving In_____

4 weeks before you move	Buy insurance.	Visit your new home. Check the fire alarms. Decide how to decorate.
2 weeks before you move	Tell the post office you are moving.	Call C&P for new service. Call a long-distance company for long-distance service.
1 week before you move	Call to arrange for: electricity/gas. water/sewage. cable TV. heating oil (if necessary). the elevator. Reserve if necessary.	
1-2 days before you move	Call the moving company to confirm all arrangements.	

Insurance

Kinds of insurance. Buy home insurance as soon as possible (see chapters on "When You Arrive" and "Finding a New Home"). You should have a:

- tenant's policy if you are renting.
- homeowner's policy if you own a home. This pays for your home if it is destroyed or damaged— for example, by fire or hurricane.

Most homeowner's plans include:

- personal property insurance. If something is damaged or stolen, the insurance company will pay part or all of the cost to replace it. If you have valuable items— such as jewelry, furs, rugs, art, and antique furniture—get a written appraisal, or value estimate, for each item.
- liability insurance. If a visitor is injured in your home, you may be legally responsible. Liability insurance will pay for any legal and medical expenses.

What to look for

Size of the company. Larger companies may be safer than smaller ones. If a company goes out of business, you may lose your coverage.

Cost. Talk to an insurance agent about:

- the deductible. This is a part of the cost the insurance does *not* pay (see chapter on "Driving a Car").
- the coverage. Find out what percentage of the total value of your house and property the insurance will pay. You may get a discount for putting in safety devices—such as burglar alarms, extra fire extinguishers, and smoke detectors.

 Compare prices for similar amounts of coverage (for sample costs, see chapter on "Finding a New Home"). When comparing, remember that some agents sell insurance for only one company. Other agents sell insurance for different companies.

Also remember that an agent may try to sell you more than you need. You may want to ask a few agents how much to buy.

Before You Move

Post office

Complete a "Change of Address" card at your local post office. Any mail

---

If you rent an apartment, report any problems or damage to your landlord or building manager immediately. If you ask for help but do not get any, call the Landlord and Tenant Commission for your area (see "Information").

sent to your old address will be forwarded, or sent, to your new home for 1 year. Send a card with your new address to any person, publication, or office that sends you mail.

C&P telephone

C&P Telephone gives service to the Washington metropolitan area, but it does not give long-distance service. For example, you need to sign up with a long-distance company to call New York City or California. For complete information about using the telephone, see the chapter on "The Telephone."

How to get phone service

1. **Decide how many phones you want and where you want them.**

2. **Call C&P Telephone's business office.**

Tell the sales representative:

- your address.
- when you want the new service connected and your current service disconnected.
- how you want your name listed in the telephone book.
- if you want an unlisted or unpublished number (see "Words to Know").

- what special services you want (see chapter on "The Telephone").

3. **Buy or lease a telephone.**

You can buy telephones from any telephone, office supply, department, or electronics store. You can rent one from AT&T; call 1-800/555-8111 or go to any AT&T phone center.

4. **Order long-distance telephone service separately from your local service.**

C&P Telephone does not offer long-distance service. Find out more about long-distance phone companies *before* you move (see chapter on "The Telephone").

 Call the C&P business office at least 3-5 business days (Monday-Friday) before you move.

 When your service is installed, you will pay a monthly fee—around $18 for unlimited (flat rate) service. To install this service, you will pay a (see "Information"):

- new service charge ($30-$50), depending on where you live.
- service call charge if you need extra lines or wires ($42-$58), plus $16 for each 15 minutes. This cost is in addition to the new service charge.
- security deposit. If you have not had a phone in this area before,

you will pay a deposit—usually around $40. You will get this money back 1 year later.

Electricity

 If you live in the District or Maryland, call PEPCO at least 3 days in advance. If you live in Northern Virginia, call Virginia Power at least 1 week in advance (see "Information").

 In Virginia, newcomers often pay a deposit of $35-$180. Maryland and District residents do not.

For a house with all electric appliances, heating, and cooling, the average monthly electric bill is $75-$250 for a three-bedroom house and $50-$100 for a one-bedroom apartment. Bills are usually higher in the summer, when people use more air conditioning.

Ask the utility company about its energy-saving programs. If you use one of these programs, you get a discount on your monthly bill.

Gas

If your home uses natural gas for heating or cooking, call the Washington Gas Company at least 1 week in advance (see "Information").

 The average monthly heating bill for a three-bedroom house is about $50. Bills are usually higher in the winter, when people use more heat.

Water and sewage

In some communities, you need to contact the local government or a private company for water and sewage service (see "Information"). Make sure your water is turned on and your house is connected to a sewer.

 The average quarterly bill (every three months) for a family of four is $110.

Heating oil

If you have an oil-burning furnace, contact a local oil supply company.

Furniture

You can buy used furniture from:

- used furniture shops.
- antique dealers.
- individuals.
  - Check the classified ads under "Merchandise Mart," "Apartment & Moving Sales," and "Garage Sales."
  - Look for yard sale signs in your neighborhood. Friday, Saturday, and Sunday are the best days. You may try to bargain at these sales.

You can buy new furniture from a department or furniture store. You can rent furniture from a furniture rental store.

Pets

All counties and cities require you to license your dog (see "Information"). Some areas require you to license a cat or other animal; some areas do not. All dogs and outdoor cats must wear tags with the date of their last rabies vaccination; otherwise, Animal Control will pick them up.

 The license fee is $10-$15. Fines for unlicensed pets are $40-$50, depending on where you live. Ask your local Department of Animal Control about:

- licensing.
- leash laws.
- vaccinations against diseases such as rabies and distemper.

Moving

 Reserve a mover 2 weeks or more before you move. If you need to move soon, try to move:

- between the 7th and 10th days of the month; you may be able to get a mover in 1-3 days.
- the middle of the month; you may be able to get a mover in about 1 week.

 The cheapest way to move is to hire a van or a truck for about $30-$60 a day and move yourself. You will pay a deposit of $120,

but you get the deposit back when you return the vehicle.

If you use a mover, start early in the morning; some movers charge more after 5 pm. The cost usually depends on the:

- number of hours worked.
- number of people working.
- weight of the furniture and boxes.
- distance between the two homes.
- driving time from one home to another.

Find out in advance how much a mover charges for services such as:

- giving you mattress bags.
- renting you wardrobe boxes.
- moving appliances.

Tip each mover $15-$20 after the job is completed.

Moving companies

Ask for:

- written estimates. Get an estimate from three to five companies. Choose one with a middle-range price.
- at least three good references.

Also be sure the mover:

- is bonded, or insured.
- has experience in international moves if you are moving from a different country.

For information on moving, you can order the pamphlet "Your Rights and Responsibilities When You Move" from the Interstate Commerce Commission: 215/596-4040

What to do

1. **Keep written records.**

Write down:

- the transit time (how long it will take).
- the itemized cost estimate, or an "order for service." If possible, get a "binding estimate" so the company cannot add a lot of extra costs.
- insurance. Be sure you know the amount of insurance that the company can provide in case of damage. You can also buy separate insurance from an insurance company.
- an inventory of each item to be moved; it should list each item separately and describe any damage or marks already on the items before the move begins.

2. **Decide where you want each piece of furniture and each box to go in your new house.**

3. **Call your mover to confirm the day and time of the move.**

4. **Reserve the elevator if you live in an apartment building.**

5. **Watch carefully during the loading and unloading of your furniture.**

After You Move

Trash collection

Local trash pick-up is usually free, but some places charge homeowners a monthly or annual fee. Ask your neighbors or call the city or county number for your area (see "Information").

If the local government does not pick up the garbage on your street, you may need to hire a private trash collector. Trash collection by a private company costs about $50 for 3 months.

Street pick-up. Put your trash in plastic bags, tightly tied at the top. Put the bags in a plastic or metal can with a lid on top. Leave the cans or bags near the street curb the night before or early in the morning (by 7 am) on pick-up day. Make sure that raccoons or other animals cannot get into the trash; if the trash is spilled on the street, the garbage service will not pick it up.

Large items. The regular trash collection service does not pick up large items—such as sofas, refrigerators, or mattresses. Call the number for your area for more information (see "Information").

Recycling. Most communities have programs to recycle newspapers, glass and plastic bottles, and aluminum cans. Ask your neighbors or call the number for your area (see "Information"). You will get a large blue plastic box; on the scheduled days, you put the box on the curb for pick-up.

Apartment buildings and condominiums. Find the trash room on your floor or for your building. Ask the building management about recycling.

Fire alarm systems

By law, every home must have a smoke detector on each floor. The detector makes a loud noise if smoke is in the air. If your smoke detector runs on batteries and makes a noise for no reason, you need new batteries. Some families replace these batteries every year—just to be sure.

You may also want to have fire extinguishers in your home—especially the kitchen. You can buy them at a hardware store.

Burglar alarm systems

Burglar alarms warn you if someone is breaking into your home. These systems are usually connected to a monitoring service. When the alarm goes off, the service gets a message and calls you. If you are not at home, the service calls the police station.

To install the alarm system, you might pay $300-$400 for an apartment and $1,500-$2,500 for a house. The monitoring service costs an additional $18-$30 per month. Whether or not you need an alarm

system depends on the area; ask your neighbors if they have one. Then decide for yourself.

Home Services

Lawn care

Even if you are renting a home, you need to take care of the lawn. You can hire a lawn-care company to do all the yard work. Some companies give discounts if many people on the same street use them.

Housekeeping

Housecleaning company. $80-$150 a day, or $15-$20 for each maid. The company will send one or more people at a time. Most cleaning companies are bonded; that is, they will pay if anything is damaged or stolen.

Individual housekeeper. $8-$12 an hour. Individual housekeepers often cost less than the companies and will do more types of jobs than other services.

Window-cleaning company. $90-$150 for cleaning all the windows in your home.

Space/Storage

Storage space. If you live in an apartment or condominium, your building manager may have a storage area you can lock, but do not use it for valuables—such as jewelry or money.

111

Self-storage services. Self-storage companies rent rooms for storing appliances, furniture—almost anything you want. You can also get "climate-controlled" rooms for items such as books and paintings.

Dry cleaners will store clothes—including furs and wool blankets—for the winter or summer. Usually, you pay for only the cleaning cost.

Shelves and closet organizers. You can buy these at many hardware and home stores. Some of these stores will help you organize your closets for free if you bring in the measurements.

"Closet stretchers." These services will organize your storage space for you. Look under "Closet Accessories" in the C&P yellow pages phone book.

Home Improvement

 When you hire an electrician, plumber, painter, or cabinet maker, you pay for:

- labor. You may pay by the hour or by the job.
- materials. You should pay a fixed price.

 If you pay by the hour or day, get a written cost estimate, but remember that the cost might be much more or less after the job is completed.

How to hire a contractor

1. **Look for a good service.**

One place to look is *The Washington Post* "Home" section on Thursdays.

2. **Check the quality of the service.**

- Get references.
- Call the Office of Consumer Affairs or the Better Business Bureau (see "Information"). Find out if the business is licensed; make sure no one has complained.

3. **Get a contract in writing.**

The contract should list:

- all the work the contractor will do.
- all guarantees and warranties.
- the price.
- any expenses you or the contractor pay for.

4. **Keep a copy for yourself and give one to the contractor.**

 All contracts are binding—that is, you cannot change your mind after you have signed the contract, but some contracts have a 3-day "cooling-off" period. If you change your mind within 3 days, the contract is no longer good.

? ***What if I lock myself out of
the house?*** Always make extra
keys to your home in case you
lose one; you can get them made at
any hardware store. If you live in an
apartment, the manager may have
another key. Otherwise, call a lock-
smith. Generally, locksmiths charge
$85-$90 per hour during business
hours (9 am-5 pm, Monday-Friday),
and $100 per hour after 5 pm and on
weekends.

Information

Telephone

DC

- English: 202/346-1000
- Spanish: 202/508-2303

MD

- English: 301/954-6260
- Spanish: 301/954-6250

VA

- English: 703/876-7000
- Spanish: 703/280-4652

Electricity

- PEPCO: 202/833-7500
- Virginia Power: 703/934-9670

Gas

- Washington Gas (DC, MD, and
VA): 703/750-1000

Pets/Animals

DC: 202/576-6665

MD

- Montgomery County
Gaithersburg: 301/258-6343
Rockville: 301/309-3115
All other areas: 301/279-1095
or 279-1823
- Prince George's County: 301/
499-8300

VA

- City of Alexandria: 703/838-
4775
- Arlington County: 703/931-9241
- Fairfax County
Rabies vaccinations: 703/830-
1100
Dog licenses: 703/830-1103

Trash collection

DC

- Regular: 202/727-4825
- Bulk: 202/576-6804

MD

- Montgomery County: 301/217-
2410
- Prince George's County
Regular: 301/952-4744
Bulk, Upper Marlboro: 301/
627-1465
Bulk, Bowie: 301/464-8400

VA

- Alexandria
Regular: 703/751-5130
Bulk: 703/370-7722
- Fairfax County
Regular: 703/550-3481
Bulk: 703/631-1179

- Arlington County
    Regular: 703/358-6570
    Bulk: 703/370-7722

Recycling

DC: 202/939-7116

MD

- Montgomery County: 301/217-2410
- Prince George's County: 301/952-4612

VA

- Alexandria: 703/751-5872
- Fairfax County: 703/324-5052
- Arlington County: 703/358-6570

Water and Sewage

DC: 202/727-5240

MD: 301/206-8000

VA

- City of Alexandria: 703/549-7080
- Arlington County: 703/358-6485
- Fairfax County: 703/698-5800

Office of Consumer and Regulatory Affairs

DC

- Consumer Affairs: 202/727-7080
- Landlord Tenant Affairs: 202/727-7315

MD

- Montgomery County
    Consumer Affairs: 301/217-7373

Landlord-Tenant Affairs: 301/217-3660
- Prince George's County
    Consumer Affairs: 301/925-4700
    Landlord-Tenant Affairs: 1-800/487-6007

VA

- Alexandria
    Consumer Affairs: 703/838-4350
    Landlord-Tenant Affairs: 703/838-4545
- Arlington County
    Consumer Affairs: 703/358-3260
    Landlord-Tenant Affairs: 358-3765
- Fairfax County
    Consumer Affairs: 703/222-8435
    Landlord-Tenant Affairs: 703/222-8435

Words to Know

Binding estimate: the amount the service costs. The company cannot charge you more than this amount.

Bonded: insured in case a worker breaks or steals something

Burglar alarm: a security system, usually with lights and an alarm, that goes on if someone tries to break into your house

Climate-controlled: a room or storage area kept at a particular temperature

Closet organizers: extra shelves and poles built into a closet to make it hold more

Contract: a written agreement between two people

Cooling-off period: usually a few days to a month when you can change you mind about a contract

Cost estimate: the amount a service will probably cost

Coverage: the type and amount of insurance you get

Deductible: an amount of money the insurance company *does not* pay

Deposit: money you pay before a service starts

Dry cleaners: a store that cleans clothes you cannot wash at home

Fixed price: a cost that does not change, usually for parts or building materials

Guarantees/warranties: written promises that something will work the way it should, or that work done will be the way you want it

Hardware store: a store that sells many items for the home—such as tools, light bulbs, door knobs, and wooden shelves

Inventory: a list of things stored, packed, or shipped

Labor: what you pay for the time it takes someone to do work

Leash laws: laws about keeping your pet on a leash, attached to you, or tied up

Liability: insurance that pays for legal and medical expenses if a visitor is injured in your home

Licensed: the contractor is approved by the government to work

License tag: a small metal tag to put on your pet's collar to show it is registered with the city

Monitoring service: a service that listens for your burglar alarm. It calls you or the police if the alarm goes on.

Personal property insurance: insurance that protects the contents of your home

Recycling: to reuse cans, bottles, plastic, and paper

Reference: a person who has used a store or services before. He or she can tell you if the service was good.

Sewage: the pipes that take water out of your house

Smoke detector: an alarm in your home. It makes a loud sound if smoke is in the air.

Unlisted number: a type of telephone number that will not be listed in the telephone book or with the "information" operator—giving you privacy

Unpublished number: a type of telephone number that will not be listed in the telephone book. The "information" operator will give someone your number.

115

___Parts of a Car___

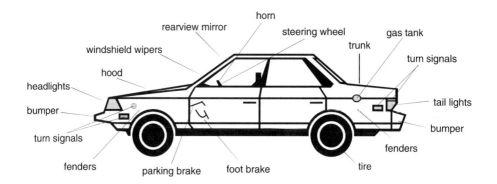

words you might hear

2-door: a car with two front doors

4-door: a car with four doors. Two doors are in the front and two in the back

4-wheel drive: a car that stays on the road better because all four wheels turn. These cars are good for muddy roads and high hills.

ABS: a safety feature that keeps the brakes from "locking." It keeps the

car from sliding when you stop suddenly.

Convertible: a car with a roof made of heavy cloth. The top can be folded back so you ride without a roof.

Hatchback: a car that has a door in the back. The door swings up, so you can put things in the open area behind the seat.

Sunroof: a window on the car's roof

Driving a Car

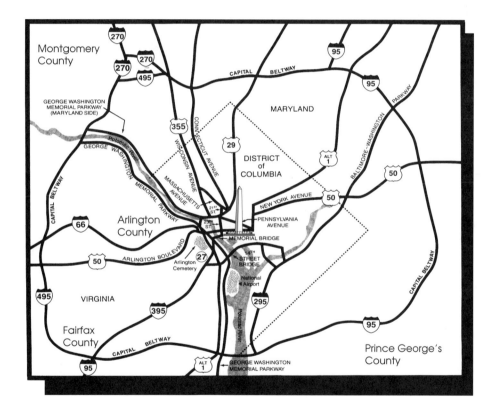

Getting a License

You need a state driver's license to drive in the U.S. You will also use this license as an identification (ID) card; you may have to show it when you write a check or apply for credit.

Get a local license at your state's Motor Vehicle Administration (MVA). Diplomats and their families can get a license at the Office of Foreign Missions (see "Information"). To get a license, you must be at least 16 years old.

Get a license within 30 days after you move here (see "Information"). DC residents can make a reservation to take the driver's test; call about 1 month in advance.

The best time is:

- in the morning.
- in the middle of the week.

Mondays and Fridays are busy; so are the first and last few days of a month and the day after a holiday.

You may be at the MVA for several hours. You will fill out forms and wait in different lines.

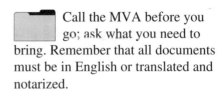
Call the MVA before you go; ask what you need to bring. Remember that all documents must be in English or translated and notarized.

You will probably need:

- an International Driver's License or a driver's license from your home country. If you have one, you may not have to take the road test (see "How to get a license").
- proof of residence. The address must be permanent; you cannot use a hotel address. Bring electricity or telephone bills with your name and address.
- proof of your name and age. Bring an original birth certificate (translated) or other official document—such as your employment authorization card.
- your passport, with your visa and I-94 card.
- Social Security card (see chapter on "When You Arrive"), if you have one.

Note: G-4 visa holders and their dependents must have a letter from the U.S. State Department Driver's Service before they go to the MVA; call the Driver's Service at 202/895-3521.

Cost of Getting a License			
	DC	**MD**	**VA**
Learner's Permit	$ 3	$22	$ 3
Driver's License	$20	$30	$12

? *What if I do not drive?* You will need an ID card when you cash a check or apply for credit. If you do not drive, you can get a Non-Driver's Identification card at the MVA. Bring the documents listed above for getting a license; you will not take any tests.

How to get a license

1. Call the MVA in your state.
Ask:

- what you need to bring.
- the cost.
- the address of the nearest MVA office.
- how to get a driver's manual. This tells about driving and parking laws and gives sample driving test questions.
- if you can take the test in your own language.

2. Go to the nearest MVA office.

3. Fill out the application and stand in line.
Be ready to show your documents. If you have questions, go to the information desk.

4. Take these tests:

- vision. You read numbers and letters on a chart; you can wear glasses or contact lenses.
- written. You take a test about the driving and parking laws. Sometimes you take this test on a computer.
- road. An MVA official will sit in your car while you drive, tell you what to do, and watch you drive.

You might not have to take all of the tests if you have a valid:

- International Driver's License.
- driver's license from your home country.
- driver's license from another state in the U.S.

5. Pay the license fees.
You may pay by cash, check, or money order.

6. Have your photo taken.

? *What if I do not have a license from my home country?* To get a license, you must first get a learner's permit; the permit

All MVA stations have interpreters and give the test in several languages. Call the main MVA number for more information.

lets you drive when a licensed driver at least 18 years old sits next to you. The learner's permit is valid for 6 months to 1 year, depending on where you live. You must pass the vision and written tests to get the permit.

If you are under 18 years old, you must complete a driver education program (see "Information") to get your learner's permit.

? *What if I lose my license?* To get a new license, go to the MVA office in person. Bring the same documents as before. You will pay a small fee.

Rules of the Road

General rules

Driving on the right side. Drive on the right side of the road. Pass on the left.

Speed limit. This is posted on the right side of the road. If there is no sign, the general rule is:

- 25-30 miles per hour (mph), or 40-48 kilometers per hour, in business areas.

- 50-55 mph, or 80-88 kilometers per hour, on divided highways.

Stopping for a school bus. Stop if you see a school bus stopped in front of you with its lights flashing. You must stop even if you are on the other side of the road, facing the bus. Wait for the school bus to start again before you go.

Seat belts. By law, the driver and any other person in the front seat must wear lap and shoulder belts. Infants must sit in a child safety seat. Children under five must sit in a child safety seat or wear a lap belt.

Driving while drinking. The police can stop your car and test your breath for alcohol. If you have been drinking, you may lose your license, pay a fine, or go to jail.

Your license. Carry your driver's license and car registration card whenever you are driving. Keep the car registration in your wallet—not in the car—in case your car is stolen.

If you have a learner's permit, the person next to you in the car must have a license. Keep car rental documents in the glove compartment.

Note: Get a driver's manual to learn all the rules.

> In general, drive along with the rest of the traffic. Remember: you can get a ticket and have to pay a fine for driving too slow or too fast.

Roads/ Highways

Lanes

Local and express. Some highways have lanes on the right for local traffic; use these lanes if you plan to get off soon or if you drive very slowly. Express lanes are for those who want to go much farther.

High Occupancy Vehicle (HOV) lanes. Virginia has High Occupancy Vehicle (HOV) lanes for cars carrying at least three or four people at certain times of the day. (The sign will tell you how many people should be in the car.) Do not use an HOV lane if you do not have enough people; you can be fined up to $75.

Highways

U.S. (interstate) highway signs are always red, white, and blue and shaped like a shield. State highway signs are black and white.

 Highways in the Washington area are always crowded at rush hour, from 7-9:30 am and from 4-7 pm. In the morning, they are more crowded going toward the city. In the afternoon, they are more crowded going away from the city.

Major roads

The Capital Beltway (I-495/I-95) is the largest local highway in Washington; it goes for 67 miles around the city—like a belt. When you listen to traffic reports on the radio, you will hear about the inner loop (the inside lanes, closest to the city) and the outer loop (the outside lanes, farthest from the city).

Shirley Highway (I-395) goes north and south from the southern part of the Beltway in Virginia to downtown Washington. It goes from the District to parts of Alexandria and Crystal City.

Custis Parkway (I-66) goes from Front Royal, VA to downtown Washington.

George Washington Memorial Parkway runs alongside the Potomac River from Mt. Vernon to McLean, VA. It has two lanes in each direction and is very scenic.

I-270 goes from the Beltway to Frederick, MD. Some parts have five lanes in each direction, with both local and express lanes. This is the best route to Rockville, Gaithersburg, and western Maryland.

I-95 goes north through Maryland to Baltimore, Philadelphia, New York City, and as far as the Canadian border. It goes south through Virginia as far as Florida.

Route 267/Dulles Access Road is a toll road that goes from Falls Church, VA, to Dulles International Airport. If you are going to Dulles, use the Dulles Access Road next to it; there is no toll.

? **What if my car breaks down on the highway?** Pull over to the side of the road. Turn on the four-way flashers, or hazards, and keep your seat belt fastened in case someone hits your car.

Raise the hood of your car and tie a white handkerchief (if you have one) around your door handle; this tells other drivers to radio or call the police. Stay in your car with the doors locked until the police come.

If you belong to the American Automobile Association (AAA), try to get to a phone and call the AAA for help; someone will come right away (see "Information").

Parking

 Your car may be ticketed or towed away if you park illegally.

Places to park

Garages. Garage parking in DC costs about $3.25 an hour, or $8-$10 a day.

Visitors' lots. If you are parking near a university or large office building, look for the signs that say "Visitors" or "Guest Parking." These are free.

Meters. Parking meters cost 25¢-$1.00 per hour, depending on where you park. You can put quarters and sometimes dimes and nickels in them.

Usually, you cannot use meters during rush hour (Monday-Friday, 7-9:30 am and 4-6:30 pm). In most places, you can park for free:

- after 6:30 pm.
- on Sundays.
- on holidays.

Parking validation. At some restaurants, stores, or movie theaters, you can park for free when you shop or buy something. Ask someone to validate, or "stamp," your parking ticket. Give the ticket to the parking attendant when you leave.

Service Stations

$ Gasoline costs about $1.05-$1.50 per gallon, depending on the time of year, the kind of gas, and where you buy it. If you are using self-service, you may have to pay for the gas before you pump it.

Some stations will give you a discount for paying with:

- cash.
- the station's credit card.

Full service means the attendant will pump the gas, wipe the windshield, and check the oil, if necessary.

Self-service means that you pump the gas yourself. The self-service price is less than the full service.

Accidents

How to handle an accident

1. **Stop immediately and get out of the car if you are not hurt.**

Do not leave the scene of the accident.

2. **See if anyone is hurt. Look for damage on both cars.**

3. **Call 911 for an ambulance or the police.**

You will need the police if either car is damaged. Ask them to write a report of the accident. Wait there until the police arrive; it may take 15-30 minutes.

4. **Write down information from the other driver.**

This includes the driver's:

- name.
- telephone number.
- insurance company.
- license plate number.

Write down this information even if you do not see any damage; you may have a problem with the car at a later time.

5. **Write down the names and telephone numbers of any witnesses (people who saw the accident).**

Later, you may need to call them and ask them to tell the police or insurance company what they saw.

6. **Call your insurance agent or company as soon as you can.**

Call even if you are far from home.

7. **Save all bills for car repairs or medical care.**

You will need to give these to your insurance company.

8. **Call the non-emergency number for the police (see "Information").**

See if you need to fill out any forms for minor accidents.

Dial **911** for an ambulance or for the police or fire department.

Information

Office of Foreign Missions

3507 International Place, NW, Washington, DC. 202/895-3512

Motor Vehicle Administration

DC: 202/727-6680

Road test: 202/727-6580

Test hours: Monday, Tuesday, Thursday, Friday, 8:15 am-3:00 pm; Wednesday, 8:15 am-7 pm.

MVA station: 301 C St., NW.

MD: 301/950-1682

Road test: 301/950-1682

Test hours: Monday-Friday, 8:30 am-4:30 pm; Saturday, 8:30 am-12 pm.

MVA stations:

- Montgomery County: 15 Metropolitan Grove Rd., Gaithersburg. 301/948-3177
- Prince George's County: 10251 Central Ave., Upper Marlboro. 301/350-9771

VA: 703/761-4655

Road test (call 2 days before you want to take the test): 703/875-0136

Test hours: Monday-Friday, 10 am-8 pm, Saturday, 9 am-2 pm.

MVA stations:

- Alexandria: 930 N. Henry St.
- Alexandria (Franconia): 6308 Grovedale Dr.
- Arlington: 3411 S. Fifth St.
- Fairfax: 5815 Seminary Rd.
- Vienna: 1968 Gallows Rd.

Driver education courses

DC: 202/829-1959

MD

- Montgomery County: 301/929-2025
- Prince George's County: 301/386-1543

VA: no public courses offered.

Non-emergency police

DC: 202/727-1010

MD: 301/424-2101

- Montgomery County: 301/279-8000
- Prince George's County: 301/336-8800

VA: 703/323-4500

- Alexandria: 703/838-4444
- Arlington County: 703/558-2222
- Fairfax County: 703/691-2131
- Falls Church: 703/241-5054

Words to Know

American Automobile Association (AAA): a club for car drivers. It provides services—such as emergency repairs.

Beltway: the main highway around the District

Child safety seat: a car seat for a small child

Divided highway: a highway with grass, land, or a wall in the middle

Driver education: classes for people who want to learn how to drive and get a license

Driver's manual: a book that tells about driving and parking laws and gives sample driving test questions

Full service: complete gas station service

Gallon: 3.8 liters

Glove compartment: a small storage space in the dashboard of the car

Hazards: flashers; emergency lights on the side and back of a car

High Occupancy Vehicle (HOV) lane: a lane for cars with three passengers or more

Inner loop: the inside lanes of the Beltway

Learner's permit: temporary driver's license used until you pass the final driving test

Meter: a machine on the side of a road. You must put money in the meter to park your car there.

Motor Vehicle Administration (MVA): the state agency in charge of all traffic and auto regulations

Non-driver identification card: an identification card given by the MVA to people who do not drive

Notarize: to make a document legal; to put an official stamp on a document

Outer loop: the outside lanes of the Beltway

Registration card: a card that proves your car is registered by the Motor Vehicle Administration

Rush hour: the time of day when most people are driving to or coming home from work

Seat belts: safety belts attached to the car seats. You must wear seat belts in MD, VA, and DC.

Self-service: to pump your own gas

Validation: a stamp on your parking ticket that gives you free or discount parking

Buying a Car

Minivan: *$15-$28,000*

Convertible: *$13,000 and up*

Cargo van: *$13-$18,000*

Sportscar: *$13,000 and up*

Sport/Utility vehicle: *$14,500-$38,000*

Sedan: *$10,000 and up*

Getting the Best Price

$ The list price, or "sticker" price, is different for each car and for each dealer. In general, it varies with the make, model, size, and general features of the car.

New car prices

These prices depend on:

- the factory invoice price, or price the dealer paid.
- the dealer's mark-up, or profit added to the factory invoice price. Each dealer adds a different amount, so you must compare. In general, the dealer's mark-up is about 12%-15% of the factory invoice price.
- extras. You may pay more for extras—such as air conditioning or a sunroof. These should be listed on the sticker price.
- warranties. With a warranty, the dealer will fix any major problems—for free or at a discount.

Used car prices

These prices also depend on:

- the person or business you buy it from. Cars sold by dealers usually cost more.
- warranties. Cars sold by dealers usually come with a warranty; cars sold by individuals usually do not.
- the model year. Of course, newer cars cost more than older ones.
- mileage, or the number of miles the car has been driven. By law, the mileage must be on the odometer of every car—either used or new.
- condition. If you are buying a used car, have a mechanic inspect it (see below).

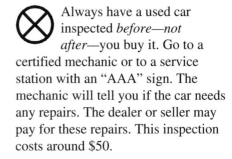 Always have a used car inspected *before—not after*—you buy it. Go to a certified mechanic or to a service station with an "AAA" sign. The mechanic will tell you if the car needs any repairs. The dealer or seller may pay for these repairs. This inspection costs around $50.

Some dealers have a "single-price policy"; that is, you may not negotiate or get a lower price. Bargain with all other dealers. Do not start bargaining unless you really want the car, but you do not have to buy the car if you and the dealer cannot agree. *Remember:* you can change your mind at any time before you sign the contract.

Other costs

In addition to the price of the car, you will pay other costs, including:

- dealer preparation, or what the dealer does to make the car ready to drive—such as cleaning and testing. Dealers often charge $50-$70.
- insurance (see "Insurance").
- taxes. The taxes are
  - DC: 6%-7%.
  - MD: 5
  - VA: 3%.
- title and registration fees (see "Registration").
- a car inspection fee.

How long it takes

If the dealer already has the car you want, you may be able to take it home right away—if you already have insurance. If the dealer has to order the car with special colors or features, you may wait 6 or more weeks.

Getting information

Before you negotiate the price, find out:

- the factory invoice price for new cars.
- the recommended price for used cars.

You can get these prices from special services or from books and magazines at the library. Many credit unions also have books on car prices for their members. Also, Montgomery County has a useful booklet called *Bumper to Bumper, A Consumer's Guide to Car Buying.* For a copy, call the Office of Consumer Affairs. 301/217-7373

How to buy a car

1. **Compare the prices at several auto dealers.**

When you enter the showroom, a dealer will ask if you need help. To look around by yourself, say, "I'm just looking, thank you."

2. **Ask questions.**

It is not impolite to ask a lot of questions and then say, "I want to look around some more" or "I want to think it over."

3. **Test drive the car.**

The dealer will let you take a short drive in the car.

4. **Bargain for a good price if the dealer does not have a single-price policy.**

Tell the seller you know the factory invoice or the recommended price. Also tell the seller what price you expect to pay.

5. **Get a bill of sale *in writing* before you buy a car.**

The bill of sale tells the price, the make and model of the car, and all the extras.

6. Discuss financing.

If you discuss financing with the dealer, check out the terms with banks and other lenders.

7. Pay for the car or make a down payment.

You may pay with:

- a credit card. You will probably pay with a credit card if you have one, but the dealer may charge about 3% extra—the amount dealers usually pay the credit card company.
- cash. Many dealers do not like cash.
- a check. Many dealers prefer a certified check.

Insurance

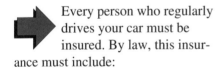 Every person who regularly drives your car must be insured. By law, this insurance must include:

- liability insurance for damage done in an accident to the other car or for injuries suffered by people in the other car.

- collision insurance for the damage to your own car.

To buy insurance, you need a U.S. driver's license. Most companies require a U.S. driver's license. The American Automobile Association (AAA) gives insurance to internationals who have a certain type of visa and an International Driver's License; newcomers can get this insurance for 1 year.

A no-claim letter from your home insurance company may help to reduce your rate. This letter says that you are a safe driver. If you do not have one, you will be called a "high-risk" driver, and your rates will be higher.

Compare the prices and benefits of a few different companies. Some agents sell insurance for only one company; others sell insurance for different companies.

Insurance can be very expensive—especially for newcomers to the U.S. For example, liability insurance alone may be:

- $690 for diplomats.
- $744 for non-diplomats.

Check with an insurance agent to see how much coverage you should get.

Before you can drive the car, you must:

- have the car inspected (used cars only).
- get automobile insurance.
- register the car. The dealer will give you temporary license plates until you get permanent ones.

Premium

The yearly cost of insurance (the "premium") depends on the:

- type and condition of the car.
- age and sex (male or female) of the driver(s).
- amount and type of coverage you get.
- amount of your deductible. This is the amount you must pay for repairs before the insurance company starts to pay. The higher your deductible, the lower your insurance payments.
- area you live in.
- amount of time you have lived in the U.S. If you have been here less than 2 years, your insurance may be higher.

Lowering the price

To lower the price of your insurance payments, ask about:

- a higher deductible. You will pay more if you have an accident, but you may decide to take that chance.
- discount policies. For example, you might get a discount for having an alarm system or air bags in your car.
- using the same agent for your home and car insurance.

To learn more, call the Insurance Information Institute (see "Information").

 What if a friend drives my car and has an accident—am I still insured? Yes.

Registration

If you buy the car from a dealer, the dealer will register the car and send away for the car title, or paper that shows you own the car. If you buy from an individual, go to the nearest Motor Vehicle Administration (MVA) office.

 The costs of registering your car range according to where you live:

- DC: $50-$83 for registration; $20 for the title.
- MD: $27-$50 for registration; $1-3 for the title.
- VA: $26-$31 for registration; $10 for the title.

Call your state's MVA to ask what to bring. Most offices need photo ID and fees. You will pay for:

- taxes.
- a title fee.
- a tag or registration fee.

The procedures for diplomats are different. Call the Office of Foreign Missions to find out what to do (see "Information").

- a lien recording fee, if yourcar is being financed.
- a bill of sale. For a new car, also bring the manufacturer's statement of origin, which the dealer will give you. For a used car, bring the title from the former owner.
- a lien contract if your car is being financed.
- the name and number of your car insurance policy.
- a photo ID.

Inspection

By law, you must have your car inspected for:

- safety, including lights, brakes, and signals.
- emissions, or the amount of pollution coming from your car.

In Maryland and Virginia, look for a station with a sign that tells you the station is an official "Vehicle Inspection Station." In the District, go to one of the two authorized stations (see "Information").

 All used or imported cars must be inspected. A notice about what to do will come with your registration papers.

The best time to go to the inspection station is Thursday or Friday afternoon. Try not to go during the last week of the month, when the stations are busy.

 When you go the inspection station, you will need:

- your car registration.
- your safety inspection notice.
- your emissions inspection notice.
- Bring cash. The cost is:
  - DC: $10 total for safety and emissions together.
  - MD: $35 for safety; $8.50 for emissions. Cash only.
  - VA: $10 for safety; $13.50 for emissions.

Information

Insurance Information Institute

1-800/942-4242

Office of Foreign Missions

3507 International Pl., NW, Washington, DC. 202/895-3512

Motor Vehicle Administration

Call for general information or information about registering your car (see "Information" section in chapter on "Driving a Car").

Local tags.

- Alexandria: 703/838-4560
- Arlington County: 703/358-3078
- Fairfax County: 703/691-3094

Inspection

DC

- 1827 West Virginia Ave., NE. 202/576-6392
- 1001 Half St., SW. 202/727-6816

MD

- Safety inspection at any authorized station; make an appointment.
- Emissions inspection (for information on the stations closest to you): 1-800/638-8347

VA: At any authorized station; do not make an appointment.

Words to Know

American Automobile Association (AAA): a club for car drivers. It provides services—such as emergency repairs.

Bill of sale: a document that tells the price, make, and model of the car

Collision: insurance for damage to your car because of an accident

Contract: a written, legal agreement between two people or businesses

Coverage: the kind or amount of insurance you have

Dealer preparation: what the dealer does to make the car ready

Deductible: an amount of money the insurance company *does not* pay

Down payment: the money you pay when you buy the car. You borrow the rest (see "Financing").

Emissions: gases that come from driving a car

Factory invoice price: the price the dealer paid for the car

Financing: getting a car loan from a bank or dealer

Inspection: a safety check on the car. All cars must pass inspection.

Liability: car insurance that pays for medical treatment of persons who may be injured while in your car

Lien contract: a document that shows the car is yours and who financed it

Lien recording fee: money that you pay the Motor Vehicle Administration to record that your car was financed

List (sticker) price: the price pasted on the car window while it is in the dealer's showroom

Make of a car: the company that makes the car—such as Ford or Chevrolet

Mark-up: the amount of money the dealer adds to the price of the car after the car comes from the factory

Mileage: the number of miles the car has been driven

Model: the style of car—for example, Ford Taurus station wagon or Toyota Celica GT

Model year: the 12-month period when a new model is sold—usually starting in September

No claim letter: a letter from your car insurance company that says you are a safe driver

Odometer: the meter that shows how many miles have been driven

Premium: the yearly cost of insurance

Registration: listing your car with the state

Single-price policy: a policy that sets the price for a car. You cannot bargain to lower the price.

Sunroof: a window in the car's roof

Test drive: a chance to drive the car before you buy it

Title: a document that says who owns the car

Warranty: a guarantee that your car will work. If it doesn't, you can get it repaired for a discount or for free.

English as a
Second Language

What to Learn

 Basic English

 Conversation

 Reading and writing

 Words for work

 Test of English as a Foreign Language (TOEFL)

ac-cent
(ak´sent) **Accent reduction**

How to Learn

Classes   **Books**   **Tapes**   **TV**   **Phone**

Learning English

Kinds of classes

Group classes may have two to 15 students in each class.

Private (individual) lessons are for those who want to learn alone with a teacher.

Home-stay programs let you live with an American family for 2-6 weeks.

Places to learn

Community colleges. All the local community colleges and the University of the District of Columbia have English as a Second Language (ESL) courses (see chapter on "Higher Education"). These courses sometimes take place in churches, other schools, or community centers.

You can take English classes for:

- credit. Credit courses count toward a college degree. These courses are in the college's regular catalog. You usually need to be enrolled at the college in order to take them.
- non-credit. These courses do not count toward a degree, but often you get a certificate, which may help you get a job. These courses are listed in the "Continuing Education" or "Adult Education" catalog. You do not need to be

accepted into the university to take them.

Courses at community colleges cost less for residents of the county or city than for non-residents. For example, a 15-credit course (about 80 sessions) at Northern Virginia Community College costs:

- $615 for residents of Northern Virginia.
- $2,130 for non-residents.

A non-credit program at Montgomery College costs:

- $780 for residents of Montgomery County.
- $1,500-$2,000 for non-residents.

Other expenses may include books and materials; these may cost $50-$100 per course, depending on the number of classes in the course and the type of material needed.

Public schools. Some public school systems offer ESL classes. For example, Fairfax County Public Schools offers separate ESL classes for speakers of Spanish, Korean, and Vietnamese. The City of Alexandria has four levels of English classes. Call your local high school or look for information on these courses at the library.

Usually, courses at public schools cost less than either college or private classes. For example, 70 hours of classes in the City of Alexandria course cost about:

- $45 for Alexandria residents.
- $70 for non-residents.

Private language schools. Private schools offer a greater number of courses at more flexible times during the week.

Each private school has a different price, but group classes with four to 12 students generally cost $5-$12 an hour. Individual, or private, classes cost about $20-$40 an hour.

Home study. You can learn from:

- books. Most large bookstores and some travel and foreign-language bookstores have books for learning English. Most major libraries have a variety of these books that teach English at different levels.
- tapes. If you read English well, but want to improve your listening, try "books on tape." You can listen to these books at home or in the car. Also look for them at the library.
- videos. One interesting way to improve your English is to read the subtitles for movies or operas in your own language.
- a course by phone from one of the private language schools. You will get books and sometimes other materials from the school. The teacher gives you the lessons by phone.
- individual (private) lessons. Some private schools have instructors who come to the students' homes for an extra fee. Usually, the fee depends on how far away your home is from the school. You will pay the cost of a private, or individual, lesson ($20-$40 an hour), plus the instructor's traveling time.

What to look for

Programs. Do the courses offer exactly what you want? Are they credit or non-credit?

Materials. Are they complete? Can you take them home?

Methods. For example, does the class have mostly reading and writing or mostly conversation?

Schedule. Are the class times convenient for you? When does the next class begin?

Class size. How many students does each teacher have?

Testing. Does the school give tests to decide which level is best for you? Do you take a test at the end to see what you have learned?

Teacher's training. Do the teachers have degrees in teaching or certification in ESL? How long have they taught this kind of program?

Beginning English

Immersion classes. If you want to learn a lot in a short period of time, you can take immersion, or intensive, classes. These meet 6 or more hours a day, 5 days a week. The course may take about 10 weeks. Most schools offer continuing courses.

Semi-intensive classes meet for 1-3 hours a day, 5 days a week. Other classes meet less often—for example, 1 or 2 times a week.

Conversational English classes are for people who can read and write but need to practice speaking.

Advanced English

Vocabulary courses usually teach idioms, common expressions, and the meaning of word parts.

Reading and writing courses help you read more quickly, organize your writing, outline texts, use punctuation, and spell.

Public speaking courses help you speak more clearly and in more formal situations—such as in a business meeting or presentations.

Culture tours help you learn about the U.S. and Washington while you are learning English. Look for a class with tours of DC, visits to museums, and shopping trips.

Skills for the workplace (also called English for Specific Purposes, or ESP). Some schools or centers teach words used for a specific subject or job—such as law, business, computers, economics, or medicine. You can take these classes privately or in a group. Other schools teach work skills along with English—for example, accounting, typing, and word processing on the computer.

TOEFL

You may have to take the Test of English as a Foreign Language (TOEFL) to get into a high school or college or to get a job that requires good English skills. The same schools that teach ESL usually have TOEFL courses. Test preparation companies also can help.

 The TOEFL is offered 6 times a year on Saturdays in August, October, November, January, March, and May.

Test centers. You can take the TOEFL at test centers in 170 countries across the world and in all the U.S. states. To get a free list of these centers, call the TOEFL office and ask for the TOEFL *Bulletin of Information* (see "Information").

TOEFL classes help:

- beginners to pass the test.
- advanced students write research papers and business letters and how to give speeches.

Accent Reduction

 Many foreigners can read and write English well but want to sound more "American."

What to look for

An evaluation. The evaluation will tell you how much you can improve and how much time you need.

Qualified teachers. They should be certified as ESL teachers or as speech teachers with a specialty in ESL.

Books, tapes, or other materials to take home.

Small class size. A good class should have 5-10 students.

Three to 5 or more class hours a week.

Translation Services

People go to a translation company when they need a written document translated from one language to another. Examples of official documents you may need translated are:

- school records.
- medical records.
- birth certificates.
- a license to practice a certain profession.

Translation jobs can take from 1 day to several weeks, depending on the length of the document. Most agencies will offer a "rush" service if you need it quickly, but prices are higher.

Most translation companies estimate the cost of translating a document per every thousand words, but some may charge by the word or page. Prices are $100-$400 per thousand words. The price of the whole document also depends on the:

- languages used. For example, languages such as Spanish and French are more common in this area, and translating them is generally cheaper than translating languages such as Chinese or Urdu.
- type of document. For example, a document with a lot of technical language dealing with specific subject matter (such as medical or legal terms) will be more expensive.
- length of the document. Usually there is a minimum cost for any document, regardless of its length. Also, you may be able to get a cheaper rate for longer documents.

What to look for

A general cost estimate. Remember that most companies do not give estimates before they see the document.

Notarized documents. Some companies can notarize documents, or put on a legal stamp, if necessary.

Extra help in case you have a problem with the translation or the service is not satisfactory.

Client references or sample translations.

Other services

Translation companies may sometimes also offer other language services, such as:

- interpretation services for help with speaking or listening at

143

conferences, meetings, and seminars. An interpreter can also be hired as a guide to accompany a foreign visitor around the area.

- audio tape transcriptions for transcribing (writing) a recorded tape in a foreign language or from one language to another.
- videotape dubbing for recording voices in any language over a film.
- language instruction (see "Learning English").

Information

Community colleges and public schools

See "Information" section in chapter on "Higher Education."

TOEFL

Educational Testing Service, TOEFL Office, P.O. Box 6151, Princeton, NJ 08541. 609/951-1100

Words to Know

Accent reduction: changing the way you speak so that others can better understand what you say

Certificate: a document that you get for finishing a class or course of study

Community college: a public, 2-year college that gives associate's degrees

Conversational English: a class where you practice speaking, not reading and writing

Credit: a unit of academic study that will help you get a degree

Dubbing: recording voices in any language over a film or videotape

Immersion (intensive) class: a class that meets for several hours a day, 5 days per week

Interpreter: a person who repeats someone else's words in another language

Non-credit: courses that do not count toward a college degree

Notarize: to make a document legal

Semi-intensive class: a class that meets a few hours a day, 5 days a week, or 1-2 times a week

Subtitle: words at the bottom of a movie in another language

TOEFL (Test of English as a Foreign Language): a test of your listening, grammar, reading, vocabulary, and writing skills in English

English Instruction/ Accent Reduction

Lado International College. 1550 Wilson Blvd., Garden Level, Arlington, VA 22209. 703/524-1100. English & foreign lang. Near Metro.

Communication Associates—Steve Shevitz. 8220 Canning Terrace, Greenbelt, MD 20770. 301/345-9191. Speech language therapy services.

Academic, Conversation, Workplace

TOEFL Tutoring

Experienced, Qualified Instructors

Small Group and Individual Tutoring

Reasonable Rates

Classes in Your Home Can Be Arranged

For more information call: (202) 342-1463

English Language Services

___Finding Work___

Ana Maria Castillo

222 Rockcreek Road, Arlington, VA 22052
703/999-2345

OBJECTIVE

To develop and implement training programs.

EDUCATION

M.A. Linguistics. University of Buenos Aires, Argentina, 1985.
B.A. Spanish Literature. University of Buenos Aires, Argentina, 1983.

WORK EXPERIENCE

9/88-5/91. U.S. Agency for International Development, American Embassy, Buenos Aires, Argentina. Training Coordinator.

- Developed a staff-development training program using resources from within the Mission and Third World countries.
- Designed and executed workshops on subjects such as management and interpersonal communication.

8/85-6/88. The American School, Buenos Aires, Argentina.
Spanish Program Coordinator.

- Developed curricula for Argentinian and Third World children in pre-kindergarten through 4th grade.
- Trained incoming Spanish teachers.

LANGUAGES

Native Spanish; fluent English; working knowledge of French.

REFERENCES AVAILABLE UPON REQUEST

Making It Legal

Who can work

If you are changing jobs or getting a new job, you may need to contact the Immigration and Naturalization Service (see the "Information" section in the chapter "When You Arrive").

By law, you can find a job if an employer will sponsor you, but some jobs are easier than others for internationals to get. For example, professional jobs are much easier to get than jobs for secretaries, receptionists, or clerks. Also, people with technical expertise are in the most demand. Jobs in mathematics and engineering are easier to get than jobs in the arts, law, or medicine.

Professionals with jobs often can get work authorization for several years. If your employer is willing to be your sponsor, you also may be able to become a permanent resident with a "green card." Talk to an attorney if you plan to stay longer than the date on your visa or if you plan to change jobs—even within the same organization (see chapter on "Your Legal Status").

Students (F-1) cannot work the first year. After the first year, you probably can work as long as you follow certain rules; check with the international students' office at your school. In general, you can work:

- on campus—up to 20 hours a week during the school year and full-time during vacations and holidays.
- off campus—up to 20 hours a week during the school year and full-time during vacations and holidays. The international students' office may help you find a company that has employed internationals before and is willing to do the paperwork.
- during vacation and after you graduate—for a total of 12 months; the work should be related to your studies.

Spouses. The rules for spouses vary, depending on the type of visa. For example:

- spouses of diplomats. Some countries have agreements with the United States; that is, you can work in the United States, and American diplomatic spouses can work in your country.
- spouses of international organization employees. Organizations such as the World

Getting the Immigration and Naturalization Service's (INS) approval can take 2-3 months or longer.

Bank, International Monetary Fund, or the Organization of American States can sponsor you if you find a job. Check with the right office before taking the job.

- other spouses. The rules vary. For example, G-4s may not work at certain types of job—such as grocery store cashier. Find out from the employee's organization what you can do and where to apply.

Documents you need

Legal documents. These depend on your type of visa. Ask your employer, the international students' office at your school, or an attorney.

Remember that some employers may be afraid of the law or of the paperwork. You might be able to get the job more easily if you tell an employer the steps to take.

Proof of qualifications. To prove that you are qualified, bring:

- translated diplomas/transcripts.
- training certificates from vocational-technical training programs.
- occupational licenses. Some professions need state licenses. To get the license, you need to take an exam. Contact the state licensing board.
- samples of your work. For example
  - writers. Bring samples of books or pamphlets you have written.
  - artists and illustrators. Bring your portfolio.
  - interior decorators. Bring photographs or drawings of rooms you have designed.
- copies of awards and honors received.

Looking for a Job

How to look

1. Complete the necessary legal forms.

2. Write your résumé and get samples of your work.

3. Get counseling if necessary.

4. Look into job opportunities in your area (see "Job counseling services").

5. Call a possible employer.

You might say, "Hello, my name is Ana Maria Castillo. I am calling in response to the ad for a Spanish translator. Is the job still available? How can I apply?"

6. Send a cover letter and your résumé.

7. Have an interview.

Where to look

Want ads. Read the "Help Wanted" ads in:

- the classified section of the newspaper every Sunday.
- the "Professional Opportunities" listing in the Monday business section of *The Washington Post* (for advanced professional positions).
- the *Washington Business Journal*.

Employers. Find out which companies may have the kinds of jobs you want. Look in the yellow pages and directories at the library. Ask each company if it:

- has the kind of job you want.
- is hiring or plans to hire soon.

If the answer is "yes," ask for an interview.

Networking. Talk to as many people as possible about your job interests and keep a list of possible contacts. Talk to friends, relatives, business associates, and neighbors.

Associations. If you join an association or professional organization, you will meet others in the same profession. Look in *The Encyclopedia of Associations* at the library for a list of associations. Call the main office of the association you want to join and ask for the number of the local branch or group that meets in the Washington area.

Most associations have:

- meetings about once a month.
- conventions where people come from all over the country.
- training workshops where you can learn more about your field.

Job counseling services

Schools and colleges. Vocational schools, community colleges, and universities usually have a job counseling, placement office, or career center. Also, talk to a counselor in the international students' office. Generally, colleges provide free job services to their students, including:

- self-assessment testing, which helps you plan your career.
- a career reference library, which has books on how to look for a job and on the kinds of jobs you can get.
- job listings. Government agencies and private companies send in descriptions of the jobs they offer.
- help in writing your résumé. Some career centers keep a copy of your résumé and send it to possible employers.
- on-campus recruitment programs. Employers visit the campus and talk to students.

The Continuing Education or Adult Education Department of many colleges also offers classes for people who want to find a job or start a career. These classes include:

- résumé writing.
- finding the best career for you.

- improving skills you need to get a job.

The cost ranges from $30–$300. Usually, courses at community colleges and adult education centers are the least expensive; those at private universities cost more.

State and county employment service offices. Some services are free; others may cost up to $30 for one counseling session or up to $10 for a group session.

Private employment agencies. These agencies interview you and get you a job. There is usually no fee to you—just to the company that hires you.

Private counseling companies. These companies test your skills and help you decide which career is best. These programs are very expensive—as much as $1,000.

Your résumé

Your résumé (see this chapter's opener) should include:

- your objective, or the kind of job you want.

- your name, address, and phone number.
- jobs you have had. Include every relevant job you have had, how long you worked there, where the job was, and what you did (your duties). Try not to have time gaps in your résumé. Make sure every year is included.
- your education. Include undergraduate and graduate degrees and special training classes that show you can do the job.
- special skills, such as languages you speak.
- names of publications or any articles or books you have written, even in another language.
- references. Ask first if the person will agree to be a reference. You may write references (names and telephone numbers) on the résumé, or simply write "References available upon request."
- names of professional organizations you belong to.

You can find books on specific careers, methods of finding a job, how to write a good résumé, and how to interview. One good book is *Finding a Job in the United States* (NTC Publishing). Most bookstores also have books for the local area (see Appendix D, "Books to Read").

Cover Letter

June 8, 1991

Dr. Steven Smith, Director
Training Services of America
123 Apple Street, NW
Washington, DC 20000

Dear Dr. Smith:

I am writing in response to the advertisement in *The Washington Post* on Sunday, April 15, for the position of education specialist. Enclosed is my résumé and a newspaper article describing the Spanish program I developed for the American School in Argentina.

I am a graduate of University of Buenos Aires with a Master's degree in linguistics, specializing in Spanish dialects. I have had several years of experience as a coordinator and staff trainer for educational programs developing language skills.*

I look forward to speaking with you. I will call you next week.

Sincerely,

(signature)

Ana Maria Castillo
222 Rockcreek Road
Arlington, VA 22052
Enclosure

Note: The writer tells about a job that is like the one she wants.

The Interview

Getting ready

Learn as much as you can about the job before the interview.

- Prepare questions to ask the interviewer. These questions
  - help you learn more about the job.
  - show the interviewer you are interested in the job.

- Review your own skills and how they will help you do the job. You will be expected to talk about yourself and what you have done.
- Practice the interview. Find a professional or American friend to help you prepare for the interview.

 Be on time! You can even be a few minutes early, but never be late!

 When you go to the interview, take with you:

- your résumé. Even if you have already sent your résumé to the interviewer, bring it along; the interviewer may have lost it.
- the names of references. Do not give these to the interviewer unless he or she asks for them.
- sample pages of your work. Give proof of your qualifications. Bring your portfolio if you have one.
- documents that show any prizes you have won or that tell about your work.

How to interview

1. Introduce yourself when you walk in. Shake the interviewer's hand.

2. Let the interviewer decide when to start talking about the job.

Some interviewers like to start by talking about popular subjects— such as the weather, current events, sports, or international affairs. The interviewer will probably ask about your home country.

Getting a job is hard—especially for someone from another country. A professional career counselor will help you understand what to do and what to expect. For example, some will interview you for practice so you feel comfortable with American ways. Most professionals also look over your résumé and make suggestions. This help is important because the American procedures and customs may be very different from those in your country.

3. **Answer the interviewer's questions directly.**

Explain why you want the job and why you will be good at it.

4. **Ask questions.**

For example, for a job as a translator you might ask, "How long is a typical translation project?"

5. **Thank the interviewer for taking the time to see you.**

Ask when you can call to find out if you got the job.

 May I ask questions about money? It is not impolite to ask what the pay will be, but do not negotiate at this time. Wait until the employer offers you the job.

Volunteer Work

If you cannot find a job, you can stay active by:

- taking adult education classes (see chapter on "Higher Education").
- working as a volunteer.

To find information on volunteer jobs, check the local papers and the section for your county in *The Washington Post* every other Thursday for a list of groups in your area needing volunteers (see "Information").

Other places to check are:

- nearby hospitals or nursing homes.
- schools or daycare centers.
- museums needing volunteer docents (speakers and guides). Volunteers get free classes about the museum before they begin; sometimes, the classes last for several months. These classes are fun and they will give you a chance to meet interesting people.
- special interest groups or foundations working on areas such as the environment or international aid programs. Check the phone book for the names of organizations that you are interested in.

Information

Employment applications for foreigners

U.S. Department of Labor, Employment and Training Administration: 202/523-6871

U.S. Immigration and Naturalization Service (INS)

- DC and VA: 202/514-2000
- MD: 1-410/962-2065

Virginia Employment Commission, Alien Certification Office: 703/478-7210

Employment clearinghouses and career counseling

DC: 202/639-2000

MD: 301/333-5353

- Montgomery County: 301/279-1800
- Prince George's County: 301/333-5353

VA

- Alexandria: 703/823-4135
- Falls Church: 703/876-6962
- Manassas: 703/361-1126
- Sterling: 703/478-7200
- Fairfax County: 703/750-0633

Volunteer organizations

Smithsonian Institution.

- The National Museum of Natural History ("Access 2000 Science Education Project"): 1-410/514-7270
- Central Volunteer Office: 202/357-3095

DC

- DC Cares: 202/663-9207
- DC Volunteer Clearinghouse: 202/638-2664

MD

- Doing Something: 301/891-2468
- The Governor's Office on Volunteerism (for professionals in areas of education and youth services, environment, social services, elder care, public safety): 1-410/514-7270

- Montgomery County:
  Mental Health Association: 301/424-0656
  The Volunteer Center: 301/217-4949
- Prince George's County:
  The Volunteer Action Center: 301/779-9444

VA

- Alexandria Volunteer Bureau: 703/836-2176
- Arlington County Volunteer Office: 703/358-3222
- Fairfax County Volunteer and Community Center: 703/246-3460

Words to Know

Association: a group of people who have the same interests or do the same kind of work

Career center: a place at a school that has information and people to show you how to look for a job

Cover letter: a letter that you send with your résumé to apply for a job. The letter introduces you and explains the details of your résumé.

Employment agency: a company that helps you find a job

Employment clearinghouse: a place where you can look for information about jobs

Interview: a formal meeting between you and the person you want to work for

Local branch: a small office of an organization. The branch is in a different place from the main office.

Networking: meeting and talking to other people who do the same kind of work

Occupational license: a certificate from the government that says you are qualified to do a special job

Portfolio: examples of your drawings or photographs of your work

Recruitment programs: programs in which employers visit a school and interview people for jobs

Reference: a person who can recommend you for a job—usually someone who has been your manager or employer

Résumé: a CV; a document that describes your education, jobs, and qualifications (see chapter opener)

Self-assessment test: a test that helps you find out what jobs you can do well

Special interest group: a group of people with common interests—such as the environment or international relations

Transcript: a printed official copy of your educational record—the courses you took, and your grades

Vocational school: a school that gives training in practical skills—for example, carpentry or electrical work

Want ads: job advertisements in the classified section of the newspaper

Work authorization: official permission for you to work for pay

Workshop: an educational meeting—usually lasting a day or less

Your Young Child

Day care International

3425 Franklin Avenue
Falls Church, VA 22134
(703) 437-8900

Child

Name____Jung Kwon_____Nickname____John____
Sex_M_Birthday_7/24/89__Home Phone_703/203-4124_
Father's Name___Hoi Lung_Work Phone__202/627-8100_
Mother's Name____In ae__Work Phone___703/436-2301_

Emergency Information

Name of Child's Physician:____Dr. David Miller____
Phone:____703/371-5161____

Name of contact persons if parents cannot be reached (2 names)
(1) **Name:**____Peter Kwon____**Phone**_703-230-5117_
(2) **Name:**____Tae Sun Lee____**Phone**_703-230-8988_

Persons authorized to pick up child:_____
____Mother, Father, Peter Kwon, Tae Sun Lee____

Persons not authorized to visit or pick up child:
_____none_____
_____

Allergies:____Chocolate, Bee Stings____
_____

Babysitters

The cost for a student or non-professional is around $5 per hour for one child and a little more for two or three. Some young babysitters charge less. A sitter from an agency starts at $6-$7 an hour.

Where to look

Other parents. Ask your child's day care or nursery school if you can post a note on the bulletin board. Often, other parents will share their babysitter with you.

Hospital and university nursing schools. Call the school's main office or the Dean's office.

Nearby universities. Ask for the career center or student job office.

Babysitter agencies. These may cost more, but agencies can get good sitters right away.

Nannies/ Au Pairs

Overview

Nannies. A nanny takes care of your child all day. Usually, a nanny is a professional with experience and training. Some live with the child's family ("live-ins"), but others have their own home ("live-outs").

Au pairs. An au pair is usually a student from another country who comes for a year's time. Most au pairs live with the child's family.

Au pairs work an average of 45 hours during the week. The hours can be flexible, depending on what you need.

How to find nannies/ au pairs

Agencies. Professional agencies will find a nanny or au pair for a fee (see costs below). Most check work experience, personal references, child-care experience, child-care training, or first-aid training. Some also check criminal and medical records.

Nanny schools. You may get a list of graduates of nanny schools by calling the National Council of Nanny Schools (see "Information"). These nannies have special degrees in child care.

Interviews and references. Nannies will come to your house for the interview. Agencies will check the nanny's references. Ask for at least three references if you have not gone through an agency.

Make sure the person you hire has legal permission to work in the U.S. Ask to see a "green card" and a Social Security card. Penalties for hiring illegal aliens in the U.S. are very serious.

If you use an agency, you will pay placement fees. For example, you will pay an agency for nannies a registration fee of about $50 to see the names on the agency's list. If you a hire a nanny from this list, you pay the agency $1,100-$1,200.

Nanny. A "live-out" nanny is paid about $250-$400 per week. A "live-in" nanny is paid about $175-$350 per week.

You will also pay some taxes for the nanny and possibly part of her health insurance. An agency will help you determine these costs.

Au pair. When you hire an au pair, you will pay:

- insurance fees.
- airfare.
- about $150-$185 a week, tuition for classes, and spending money.

Schools/ Centers

 You can take your young child to:

Day care centers. Most are all-day, all-year care. Children can go to most day care centers at any age.

Preschools, or nursery schools. Many have half-day programs; most preschools are closed during the summer. Often, pre-schools accept children who are:

- 2 years or older.
- toilet-trained.

What to look for

When you are looking around for a school or center, go there without an appointment. You will see what the school is like on an average day.

You can get information about day care centers and nursery schools from:

- educational counselors.
- guidebooks in local bookstores (see Appendix D, "Books to Read").
- people from your embassy.

The staff's training.

- The director should have at least 2 years of college work in Early Childhood Education (ECE) and 1-5 years of experience in a child care center.
- The teachers should have some college training in early childhood education and a year's experience.

You may send your child to a co-operative (co-op). Co-ops are centers and schools where parents help share the work in and out of the classroom. In most co-ops, parents help the teacher in the classroom— anywhere from once a week to once a month. Co-ops often cost less than other centers or schools.

The staff's attitude. Do they like children? Do any speak your language?

The program. Some centers have many organized activities; others have more free play. For example, Montessori schools often have a lot of educational toys and games, with more free play than group activities. Each child is supposed to learn at his or her own pace.

Multilingual. Some schools may use two or more languages. Call your embassy for information about a school that uses your language.

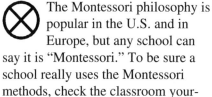 The Montessori philosophy is popular in the U.S. and in Europe, but any school can say it is "Montessori." To be sure a school really uses the Montessori methods, check the classroom yourself or call the Montessori Institute (see "Information").

The other children. Find out their:

- ages. Some centers have a wide range. Be sure there is enough care for each age.
- backgrounds. Are there other children from different countries? Are foreign languages used by the staff?

Relationship with parents. Check to see if:

- you can visit anytime.
- there are parent-teacher conferences.
- the staff welcomes suggestions from parents.

Space and equipment. Look around the whole center, inside and outside. Be sure:

- the center is clean and cheerful.
- the equipment and toys are safe.
- the outdoor play area is large and fenced.

Place. If the school or center is far away, make sure:

- the center will pick up your child for an extra fee.
- some of the parents live near you and will car pool.

Meals and snacks. Be sure the food is healthful. If your child cannot eat certain foods, find out what the center will give him or her instead.

Your child's reaction. See how your child likes the school when you visit.

Nursery schools

Calendar. The calendar is based on the school year beginning in September and ending in early June.

Each nursery school has different hours. But most run from 9 am-12 noon. Often, you can choose to send your child 2 days, 3 days, or 5 days a week. Some schools have full-day programs (7 am-6 pm) for working parents.

Class size. The class size will vary between 8-26 children; usually, it is around 14-15 students.

Who is accepted. Most nursery schools and day care centers accept whoever applies first, but there may be a waiting list. Some nursery schools look at the interview or an Intelligence Quotient (IQ) test. A few nursery schools require that the child speak or understand English.

Licensing. All good programs are licensed. To find out about a school, call the agency for your area (see "Information").

 Nursery schools usually start the year in September; if you are here in time, you might start looking about a year in advance—in September or October of the year before. Most day care centers accept children any time.

 The monthly cost is about:

- $50-$100 for 2 days a week.
- $75-$250 for 3 days a week.
- $95-$350 for 5 days a week.
- $250-$500 for a full-day, 5-day-a-week program.

How to apply

1. **Call the school to make an appointment for a visit.**

Ask if you can bring your child.

2. **Visit the school.**

Talk to the director or principal. Take a look around.

3. **Fill out an application form.**

Send it to the school, along with the application fee.

4. **Put down the names of some references if necessary.**

Give names of some people who know you or your child. Call up your references and tell them you have used their names.

5. **Have your doctor sign the school's health forms.**

6. **Take your child to the school for an IQ test if necessary.**

Most schools do not require this test.

Day care

Calendar. Day care centers operate either all year round or during the school year (from September to June).

Many day care centers are open 5 days a week, but some are open fewer days. Some centers, or "day-out" programs, let you leave your child for just one or two mornings a week.

The full-time hours are usually 7 am-6:30 pm. Half-day programs are usually from 9 am-1 pm.

 The cost for full-time day care (7 am-6:30 pm, 5 days a week) is $75-$160 a week. Morning care can cost $30-$100 a week, depending on the hours. Family day care in a private home costs about $60-$120, full-time. Infant care may cost more.

Adult/child ratio. The National Association for the Education of Young Children recommends the following ratios for adults to children in day care:

- 0-12 months, 1:4. Maximum group size: 8 children.
- 1-3 years, 1:4 (under 2); 1:7 (2-3 years). Maximum group size: 14 .
- 3-5 years, 1:7 (younger); 1:10 (older). Maximum group size: 14-20.

Licensing. To find out if a center is licensed, call the number for your area in the "Listings and information section" of "Information." In the District and Maryland, every care program should have a license. In Virginia, the counties give out licenses, but day care centers do not have to get one. Therefore, some good programs may not be registered.

Special Needs

The Childfind program is a free public service that tests for delays, or slow growth in speech/language, gross motor skills, audio/visual skills, and psychological profiles. Check with the program where you live (see "Information").

Information

Babysitting

American University, AU Career Center: 202/885-1861

Catholic University: 202/319-4480

George Mason University: 703/993-2361

Georgetown University: 202/687-4187

Howard University: 202/806-2818

Montgomery College: 301/279-5089

The University of Maryland: 301/314-8324

Nannies/au pairs: Listings and information

Child Care Aware Hot Line: 800/424-2246

National Council of Nanny Schools: 517/686-9417

U.S. Information Agency's Office of Exchange Visitor Program Services (au pair searches): 202/401-7964

American Background Information Service (conducts criminal and driver's background checks for $65): 1-800/669-2247

Day care centers and nursery schools: Listings and information

All areas.

- Department of Consumer and Regulatory Affairs: 202/727-7226
- Montessori Institute: 202/387-8020

- United Planning Organization: 202/546-7300, ext. 277

DC

- DC Childfind program: 202/724-4018
- Washington Child Development Center: 202/387-0001 or 202/387-0002

MD

- Maryland Childfind program: 301/279-3462
- Maryland Department of Education Certification and Accreditation: 1-410/333-2160
- Maryland Office of Child Care Licensing and Regulation: 1-410/333-0193

Montgomery County.

- Office of Child Care Licensing and Regulation: 301/294-0344
- Childcare Connection: 301/279-1773

Prince George's County.

- Office of Childcare Licensing and Regulation (Prince George's County only): 301/499-9790
- Childcare Referral Locate Service: 301/772-8400

VA

- Virginia Childfind: 703/876-5244
- Alexandria Child Care Office: 703/838-0750
- Arlington County Child Care Office: 703/358-5101

Fairfax County.

- Office for Children: 703/246-5440
- Child Care Resource Program (Fairfax County only): 703/359-5860

Public day care services

DC

- Department of Recreation: Year-round day care services from 7 am to 6:30 pm. 20 different locations. 202/576-7226

MD

- Montgomery County Department of Recreation: The Creative Carousel program for 3-5 year olds. 3 days a week, mornings or afternoons. 40 different locations. 301/468-4050
- Prince George's County Community Center preschool programs.
  Northern Area Office: 301/445-4500
  Central Area Office: 301/249-9220
  Southern Area Office: 301/292-9006

VA

- Arlington County Early Childhood Education: 703/358-6152
- Fairfax County Office for Children. Preschool programs in 13 Nursery Laboratory schools, mostly 3-day-a-week programs for 3-5 year-olds. 703/218-3800

Words to Know

Agency: an organization that will find a nanny or au pair for a fee

Application fee: money you pay to apply to a school

Audio/visual skills: (a child's) ability to see, hear, and speak well

Au pair: a person who lives with your family and takes care of your child

Bulletin board: a board in a public place where you can put a message

Car pool: a group of people who go in the same car

Co-operative (co-op): a day care center or school where parents share the work in the classroom

Day care center: a center where small children stay while their parents work

Day out: a day care center where you leave your child for just a few mornings a week

Gross motor skills: a child's ability to make large movements—such as running, throwing a ball, or jumping

Illegal alien: a foreigner who does not have government permission to be in the U.S.

Intelligence Quotient (IQ) test: a test that measures how smart someone is

License: a document that shows the center is approved by the government

Montessori (school): a school that has less group activities than other schools

Nanny: a person who takes care of your child all day in your home

Nursery school: a school where very young children go, usually for a half day

Parent-teacher conference: a meeting between the parent and the teacher

Preschool: a school for children who are younger than 5 years old

Psychological profile: a test that shows how someone acts and feels

Reference: a person you call to find out someone's ability to do a job

Toilet-trained: able to use the toilet; not needing diapers anymore

Waiting list: a list of people who want to join a program or school

Schools

"Spring" Bilingual Montessori Academy. Old Linden Lane, Silver Spring, MD. 301/587-3511. French, Italian, Spanish. 2½-6+ years. All year around.

Your Older Child

Elementary School

Grades	Average Age
Kindergarten	5-6
Primary	
1st	6-7
2nd	7-8
3rd	8-9
Intermediate	
4th	9-10
5th	10-11

Middle School

Grades	Average Age
6th	11-12
7th	12-13
8th	13-14

Some systems have junior high schools (grades 7-8).

High School

Grades	Average Age
9th	14-15
10th	15-16
11th	16-17
12th	17-18

The School System

 By law, children must start school at about the age of five (see "Information") and attend until the age of 16. Most attend until around the age of 18.

Most children go from one grade to the next at the end of the school year. They get report cards during the year. You, the parent, must sign this card. It tells if the child is "passing," or doing well enough to go on to the next grade.

Calendar

Most schools begin in late August or early September and end in the middle of June.

During the school year, the schools are closed for 1½-2 weeks in the winter, from the middle or end of December until around January 2. Schools are also closed for 1 week in the spring and on most national holidays.

Hours

The hours of the school day are different for each school. The day starts between 7:30-9 am and ends between 2-3:30 pm. The day is divided into class periods (30-50 minutes each) for different subjects. Students—except those in half-day kindergarten—eat lunch at school.

Public Schools

 Public schools are free for all students. They are run by either the county or city government. They accept all children.

Finding a school

Most children go to the public school assigned to their house. To find a good school before you buy or rent your home, talk to:

- a relocation center.
- a real estate agent.
- an educational counselor (see "Tutors/Counselors").

To find out which public school your child would go to, call the locator number (see "Information"). Ask if this school will be open next year.

Your child may be eligible for some special programs, such as a gifted and talented program, a magnet school, or the International Baccalaureate (see "Academic programs"). Ask the principal at your local school.

Academic programs

Levels of instruction. College-bound students must complete certain courses—such as a foreign language, algebra and geometry, and physics or biology.

Often, you can tell the level of instruction by looking at:

- Scholastic Aptitude Test (SAT) scores. The SAT is the best-known test students take to get into college. You can find out the school's scores from its office of admissions or from school guidebooks in libraries or bookstores.
- the percentage of students going to college and the colleges they attend.
- the kinds of courses offered. Most high schools have honors and Advanced Placement (AP) classes.

International Baccalaureate (IB). The IB program prepares students for the International Baccalaureate exam. Some public schools in Falls Church (VA), Montgomery County, and Prince George's County have this program—as well as several private international and embassy schools. Ask the school's guidance office if there is an IB program and how your child can get in.

Magnet schools. The District and all the counties have schools for children with special interests or talents in subjects such as foreign languages, computers, math, science, or the arts.

To find out about these magnet programs, call the number in the phone book under your county's or city's public schools. Look for the Office for Magnet Programs or the Office for Gifted and Talented Programs.

Gifted and talented. Call the Gifted and Talented number for your county (see "Information").

English as a Second Language (ESL) programs. In general, public schools have good ESL programs. Children from non-English-speaking countries take an English test before they start school so they can be enrolled in the right ESL program. You will find out where and when to go when you register your child (see "Information").

Special needs. To find out about programs for the handicapped or learning disabled, talk to the principal or director ahead of time.

If your child has trouble reading, writing, or paying attention, see if he or she can be tested for a disability. Ask:

- the principal or director.
- a private counselor.
- a learning center.

Also, see the listings under "Special needs" in "Information."

Registering your child

Non-English records must be officially translated. Some countries will translate these records for free. Bring:

- medical records, or proof that your child has had all required vaccinations (shots) and a physical exam. Often, the school can tell you where to get these vaccinations and exam for free.
- records from the school in your home country.
- birth certificate or passport.

- proof of residency (either a utility bill or copy of a document showing you rent or own a home in the area).

How to register

1. Call up the school's international student office for your school system.

Make an appointment to register your child. Find out what records and documents you need.

2. Have your child tested.

When you go to the international office, the counselor will look over your papers. Then your child will take a test in English and, sometimes, math. This test will help the teachers decide your child's program.

3. Call up the school your child will attend.

Ask about the orientation session so you can meet the principal and find out more about the school.

4. Find out about open houses.

Many schools have a an "open house," or a day to meet with all parents.

Transportation

If you do not live near the school, the school bus will take your child. Ask for a bus schedule. Find out if the school has "activity buses" for after-school programs or sports. The public school buses are free.

Academic placement

Be sure your child is in the right academic class. For example, some international students may have had different math programs in their home country. These students may be placed in remedial math classes—or classes for children having trouble understanding the work. Instead of a remedial class, the student might need a tutor.

PTAs (Parent-Teacher Associations)

Parent-Teacher Associations help you be part of the schools. Any parent can come to the meetings and join the association. In general, a strong PTA means a better school. For example, PTAs:

- raise money for school equipment or for field trips.
- talk about school matters with principals and teachers.
- hold meetings where parents get to know each other.

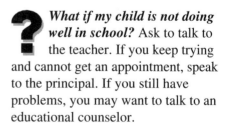

What if my child is not doing well in school? Ask to talk to the teacher. If you keep trying and cannot get an appointment, speak to the principal. If you still have problems, you may want to talk to an educational counselor.

Private Schools

 Private schools may cost between $1,700 and $10,000 a year. Most have scholarships.

Kinds of schools

Some of the kinds of private schools are:

Bilingual. These teach in English and another language. Call your embassy to find a school with your language.

International. These schools have children from many different countries—including the United States.

Religious. Some schools teach religion along with other subjects.

Special. Some schools have programs for children with special needs—such as children who are physically handicapped or learning disabled. Most of these schools also accept children without special needs.

How to look for a school

1. **Find out if the school is accredited.**

Also find out if the school is a member of a professional organization (see "Private schools" in "Information"). To be a member, a school must pass a special review.

2. **Visit the school.**

Call the admissions office and make an appointment to see the school. Ask if you should bring your child.

3. **Interview the head of the school or the director of admissions.**

Talk over the school's program.

4. **Call the school's references.**

The best references are people you know—co-workers, neighbors, or friends. You may also ask the director at your interview for names and telephone numbers of parents whose children attend the school.

 What if I need help finding the best school? Educational counselors can help. Many can give you advice about either private or public schools.

Applying for admission

If possible, contact schools a year in advance. You probably will need to send your application and school records by February 28 for enrollment the following school year.

When you apply to a private school, you will need an application fee and these records:

- a birth certificate/passport (sometimes required).
- translated school records.
- a health form signed by a doctor, which comes with the application.
- letters of recommendation from former teachers or people who know your child.
- an application fee.

What the school wants. Some schools choose only 10%-20% of the students who apply. To find out what your child's chances are, talk to the school's admissions office, to other parents and students, or to an educational consultant. Many parents apply to several schools at the same time.

Test scores. Some common tests are:

- the SSAT (Secondary School Admissions Test) for grades 5-11. This test is given in a few local private schools and in test centers around the world (see "Information").
- achievement tests (for grades 10, 11, and 12). These test skills in subjects such as languages, math, history, and science.
- the TOEFL (Test of English as a Foreign Language). This test is given in many countries. Call the TOEFL office for times and places (see "Information").

Writing samples in the child's own language. These are required by several international schools.

How to apply

1. Call the school or send a postcard asking for an application form.

2. Visit the school.

The director of admissions will meet with you and your child.

3. Have your child take a test.

Ask the admissions director what tests your child will take and when he or she will take them.

Getting accepted

Most schools mail you a letter—usually by March or April. If your child is accepted, you probably will need to send part of the tuition at this time.

Tutors/ Counselors
What they do

Private tutors and centers. Many tutors or centers teach several subjects. Some teach only reading and writing; others teach only math. Tutors may specialize in teaching English as a Second Language (ESL) or in preparing students for tests such as the SAT or SSAT.

176

Educational consultants. These consultants help:

- find the right school for your child.
- solve problems your child may be having in school.
- test your child to see
  - what he or she knows.
  - what his or her IQ (intelligence quotient) is.
  - whether he or she has some kind of learning disability.

What to look for

All tutors should be certified to teach in the state where they are teaching. Look for a special degree in one of these subjects:

- elementary education.
- the high school subject being taught, such as math or English.
- English as a Second Language.
- reading.
- special education (for children with learning or physical disabilities).

Fun Activities

School clubs

Schools offer clubs for outdoor activities and community services such as Boy Scouts and Girl Scouts; other popular clubs are science, drama, school newspaper, and international clubs such as Model U.N.

DC/county recreation

 If possible, sign up at least 2 or 3 months beforehand; the most popular classes fill up quickly.

The DC or county Department of Recreation offers programs—including sports, music, drama, and arts for children of all ages.

Call the Recreation Department for the latest programs (see the chapter opener for "Looking and Feeling Good").

 There is usually a one-time cost of about $20-$50, which includes any equipment and uniforms needed.

Information

Admissions tests

Educational Testing Service, College Board, ATP, Department E-26, P.O. Box 6212, Princeton, NJ 08541. 609/951-1100

SSAT Board, 12 Stockton St., Princeton, NJ 08540. 609/683-4440

TOEFL Office: P.O. Box 6151, Princeton, NJ 08541. 609/951-1100

Special needs

Council for Exceptional Children (a private organization for parents of handicapped and gifted children): 703/620-3660

Information Center for Handicapped Individuals: 202/347-4986

National Information Center for Children and Youth with Disabilities: 1-800/999-5599 or 703/893-6061

Hotline resources across U.S., including "Help for Children" (a booklet with comprehensive list of hotlines and resources for gifted and handicapped): 1-800/343-0686

Private schools

The Association of Independent Schools of Greater Washington: 202/462-3886

The Association of Independent Maryland Schools, P.O. Box 813, Millersville, MD 21108. 301/621-0787

The Virginia Association of Independent Schools, 101 N. Mooreland Rd., Richmond, VA 23229. 804/740-2643

Washington Small School Association, P.O. Box 32315, Silver Spring, MD 20904. 202/762-0740. Ask for Ron McLain.

Montessori Institute, 2119 S St., NW, Washington, DC 20008. 202/387-8020

The Catholic Office of Education, P.O. Box 2960, Washington, DC 20017. 202/541-3135

DC public schools

Starting age: 5 on or before December 31.

Locator numbers.

- Area A: 202/724-4168
- Area B: 202/727-2273

Note: If you do not know your area, call up either number and ask.

Gifted and talented programs: 202/767-8712

MD public schools

Montgomery County.

Starting age: 5 on or before December 31.

Locator number: 301/279-3331

Languages spoken (at office): Vietnamese, Korean, French, Spanish, Khmer, Chinese.

International Student and Admissions Office: 301/ 230-0686

Asian Hotline: 301/230-5436

Spanish Hotline: 301/230-3013

Gifted and talented programs:301/279-3391

Prince George's County.

Starting age: 5 on or before January 1.

Locator number: 301/952-6300

International students: 301/985-5164

Gifted and talented programs: 301/386-1536

VA public schools

Alexandria.

Starting age: 5 on or before September 1.

Locator number: 703/824-6600

Languages spoken (at office): Spanish.

International students: 703/ 824-6660

Arlington County.

Starting age: 5 on or before September 30.

Locator number: 703/358-6150

International students: 703/ 358-6767

Languages spoken (at office): Spanish, Cambodian, Vietnamese, Laotian, French, Chinese (Mandarin), other languages upon request.

Gifted and talented programs (general information): 703/358-6000

Fairfax County.

Starting age: 5 on or before September 30.

Locator number: 703/246-2111

Languages spoken (at office): Vietnamese, Spanish, Korean, also a language bank for other languages.

International students: 703/876-5219

Gifted and talented programs: 703/876-5272

Falls Church.

Starting age: 5 on or before September 30.

Locator number: 703/241-7600

International students: Call individual schools.

Languages spoken (at office): Vietnamese, Korean, French, Spanish, Khmer, Chinese.

Words to Know

Academic placement: the right learning level for the point at which the child is learning

Accredited: approved by the government; meeting certain standards

Achievement tests: tests used by colleges and some private secondary schools for admitting students

Advanced placement classes: classes that let a student earn college credit while still in high school. You must pass a special test at the end of the course.

College-bound: going to college

Gifted and talented: needing challenging, or higher-level, programs

Grade: a letter (A, B, C, D, or E) that tells how good the student's work is; also, a school level—such as the first grade, second grade, etc. (see this chapter's opener)

International Baccalaureate: a diploma that can be earned in addition to the regular high school diploma

Learning disabled (LD) students: students with special needs — for example, students who have trouble reading, writing, or paying attention

Magnet school: a school for students with special skills and interests

Parent-Teacher Association: a group for parents and teachers

Private school: a non-government school that students pay to attend

Public school: a school that is paid for by taxpayers and run by the city or county. Public schools are free.

Report card: a record of a student's classes and grades

SAT: a test used by colleges to decide whether to admit a high school student

SSAT: a test used by private middle or high schools to decide whether to admit a student

TOEFL: Test of English as a Foreign Language

Tuition: the cost of an educational program. The tuition does not include other expenses—such as uniforms or books and materials.

Tutor: a teacher who helps an individual student learn a specific subject

Schools

The Bullis School. 10601 Falls Road, Potomac, MD 20854. 301/299-8500. Grades 4-12. Private co-ed school.

HELLO! AMERICA BOOK ORDER FORM

NAME			
STREET			
CITY	STATE		ZIP CODE
COUNTRY	DAYTIME PHONE ( )		

	QTY	PRICE	TOTAL
Hello! Washington		**$12.95**	
"Words to Know" in Spanish (available in September) Términos útiles aparacerá en español (a partir de Septièmbre)		**$4.95**	
Add 5% sales tax (for Maryland address only)			

Shipping & Handling (choose one)

Domestic	**REGULAR (2-7 days)**	$2.00; 75¢ each additional book	
	RUSH (1 day)	$4.00; 75¢ each additional book	
Canada	**REGULAR (8-20 days)**	$5.00 per book	
	RUSH (7 days)	$7.50 per book	
International	**REGULAR (8-20 days)**	$7.00 per book	
	RUSH (7 days)	$10.00 per book	
Total Amount Due			

Payment. Call for shipping costs on bulk orders.

Make checks payable to Hello! America, Inc.

- Individuals: Orders must be prepaid, using personal checks, VISA or MasterCard.
- Individuals from outside the U.S.: Payment must be in U.S. dollars with 1) check with MICR-encoding drawn on a U.S. bank, 2) international postal money order, or 3) VISA or MasterCard.

VISA   MasterCard   Expiration Date

VISA or MasterCard Number

Signature

Print Cardholder's Name

☐ I want information on Personal Orientation Services.

MAIL! Hello! America, 7701 Woodmont Ave., #1108, Bethesda, MD 20814

PHONE! 301-913-0074   **FAX!** 301/652-4566

Higher Education

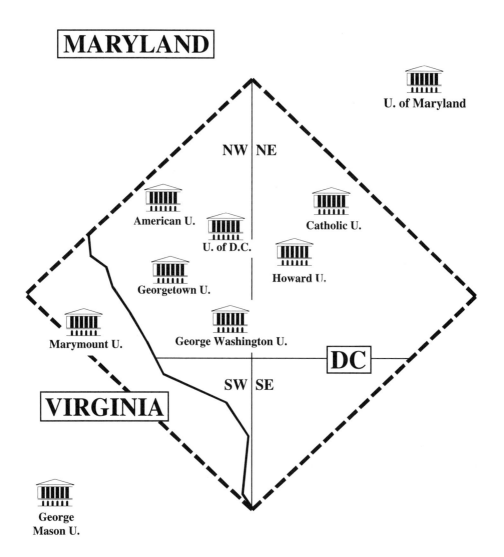

MARYLAND

U. of Maryland

NW | NE

American U.

U. of D.C.

Catholic U.

Howard U.

Georgetown U.

Marymount U.

George Washington U.

DC

SW | SE

VIRGINIA

George
Mason U.

Colleges/ Universities

Calendar

Colleges and universities offer courses for two semesters each academic year. The fall semester usually begins in early September and ends in December. The spring semester usually begins in January and ends in late May or June. Some courses are also offered during a shorter summer semester.

Each semester ends in a 1- to 2-week exam period. Vacations include 2-4 weeks in the winter and 1 week in the spring (see "Appendix A" for a list of the national holidays).

Some colleges have quarters (four sessions per year) or trimesters (three sessions per year).

Programs

Undergraduate programs.

- Associate's degree. Two-year program used for credit toward a Bachelor's degree or a training for certain jobs—such as the job of a secretary.
- Bachelor's degree. A four-year program offered at most colleges and universities. In the U.S., a Bachelor's program is usually less specialized than in other countries. The most common Bachelor's programs are the Bachelor of Arts (B.A.) and the Bachelor of Science (B.S.). You need this degree to get into a graduate program.

Graduate programs.

- Master's degree. One- to 3-year program for earning a specialized degree—for example, the Master of Arts (M.A.) or Master of Sciences (M.S.).
- Professional. Specialization in a professional field—for example the Juris Doctorate (J.D.) for practice of law.
- Doctorate. Highest degree offered by a university. Includes the Ph.D. (Doctor of Philosophy), the Ed.D. (Doctor of Education), and the Eng.D. (Doctor of Engineering).
- Post-doctorate. A non-degree program for people who already have a Doctorate but want to conduct research in a specialized area related to their degree.

Non-credit programs.

- audited courses. Classes you attend without getting a grade or credit toward a degree. You do not take any tests or write papers.

You can find more information in chapters on "Finding Work" and "English as a Second Language."

- enrichment programs. Courses for personal enjoyment or development.

Applying to College

 When you apply to college, you need:

- An application. Often, this includes an essay or "Statement of Objectives." The fee for each application is $20-$60.
- Official transcripts.Be sure to allow plenty of time to order your transcripts from your home country. Send only original copies (no photocopies!) with notarized English translations. Get
    - college or university transcripts.
    - high school transcripts (for undergraduate admission).
- Letters of recommendation from professors, advisors, or employers.
- Medical and immunization records, with English translations.
- Statement of financial ability. To prove that you are able to pay for your education, you may have to fill out a form showing how much you have and how much you owe. You may also need documents such as bank records and salary statements.

- Admissions test scores (see below).

 Submit your application materials on time—*before* the deadline. Most deadlines are in January for fall admission and in June for spring admission in the spring of the next year.

How to apply

1. **Talk to an educational counselor or your high school guidance counselor.**

A private counselor costs $60-$100 per hour. Community colleges offer free counseling for people interested in applying. A counselor will help you:

- choose the right college.
- fill out the forms.
- get help for the admissions test if you need it.
- find financial aid (see "Financial aid").

2. **Learn more about colleges you are interested in.**

- Do research. You can get many reference books with information about different colleges at bookstores or libraries. Be sure to choose books published this year.
- Read course catalogs. Call the college's administrative or admissions office and ask for a course catalog.

- Visit the campus. If possible, schedule an interview with the admissions office or with an advisor from the department you are interested in.

3. **Apply to several colleges. Most people apply to 2-10 colleges. Some colleges are hard to get into.**

Check with the college's admissions office or International Students' Office about procedures for foreign students.

4. **Have an interview.**

Schedule an interview even if the college does not require one.

5. **Take required admissions tests (see "The admissions tests").**

The admissions tests

The tests. The college's admissions office catalog will tell you which tests to take. The most common are:

- TOEFL (Test of English as a Foreign Language).
- SAT (Scholastic Aptitude Test) for undergraduate programs.
- GRE (Graduate Record Exam) for graduate programs.

Preparing. You can prepare for any of these exams by:

- getting test-preparation books and cassette tapes from a library or bookstore.

- taking a test-preparation course at a college or private institute.

 Test-preparation books cost $10-$25. For example, you can get the *10 SAT's* published by The College Board, for $11.95; the book has 10 real tests taken by students within the last few years.

TOEFL-preparation courses cost:

- $130-$200 at public school adult education centers and community colleges.
- $500-$700 at test-preparation institutes.

SAT and GRE courses cost about:

- $120-$200 at community colleges.
- $300-$350 at universities.
- $400-$700 at test-preparation institutes.

What to look for

Quality.

- Does the college have a good department for the subject you are interested in?
- Is the college accredited? You can find this out in a standard college guidebook or from the college itself.
- What resources and facilities are available—such as libraries, research centers, athletic facilities, computer centers, and career counseling?

Cost.

- How much are tuition and other expenses (see "College Costs")?
- What scholarships or loans does this college offer?

Standards.

- What kinds of qualifications (both personal and academic) do you need to be admitted?
- Is there a limit on the number of international students admitted?

Requirements.

- Which courses do you have to take?
- How many credit hours do you need to complete?
- Do you have to maintain a certain grade point average (GPA)?
- How much time do you have to finish the program?

College Costs

Costs vary from college to college; private colleges are generally more expensive than public colleges. For example, all expenses for one year (full-time) may cost:

- $4,500-$12,000 at a public college.
- $9,000-$30,000 or more at a private college.

Tuition. You pay for each credit hour. For example, if a college charges $200 per credit, a 3-credit course will cost $600. Residents get tuition discounts at public colleges and universities. For example, if you are a resident of Maryland, you will pay less tuition than a non-resident. In general, tuition at private colleges range from $12,000-$19,000 per year.

Note: These costs are for *tuition only*—not for all expenses.

Room and board. If you live and/or eat on campus, these costs range from $3,500-$6,000 per year for both private and public colleges.

Books and supplies. Costs range from $50-$200 per course.

Health fees. You will be able to use the university's medical center, counseling services, and insurance.

Student fees. These are for special activities, participation in student organizations, and use of sports facilities.

Financial aid

Scholarships, grants, and fellowships. You do not have to pay these back.

Assistantships. The college will pay you to assist a professor with research, teaching, or administrative work.

Student employment. The college will pay you to work for one of its departments or offices. Check with the Student Employment Office.

Loans. Ask the college or a private bank.

Senior citizen discounts (for older students).

Non-citizens cannot get a scholarship or loan that is paid by the federal or state government. For example, non-citizens cannot get National Merit Scholarships, but you may be able to get other kinds of scholarships. Ask your guidance counselor, a private scholarship search company, or your embassy.

Enrichment Programs

Enrichment programs offer non-degree, non-credit courses. You can take these courses during the day, evening, or weekend (see "Information").

Continuing education programs

Continuing education or adult education programs at community colleges and universities offer courses in academic, professional, or recreational subjects.

Tuition fees are $25-$160 per credit hour for residents. Non-resident tuition is 25%-50% higher. Books may cost $20-$100 per course.

Public school districts

Many public school districts offer adult education courses at a low cost to residents.

Courses cost $20-$200 for residents and more for non-residents. Some courses are free.

Public recreation departments

The recreation departments of most county and city governments offer courses and events for children and adults—such as music, dance, sports, and exercise (see chapter on "Looking and Feeling Good"). You can get a brochure at public schools, libraries, or local community centers.

Courses cost about $20-$70. Materials fees may be required for some courses.

FAES (Foundation for Advanced Education in the Sciences)

This organization at the National Institutes of Health (NIH) offers over 100 courses every year in biomedical and behavioral sciences, modern languages, general studies, and English (ESL) courses. Anyone can take these courses. The cost is $60 per credit hour ($120-$180 per course).

USDA (U.S. Department of Agriculture) Graduate School

The USDA Graduate School has over 1,000 courses in 50 subject areas—

such as foreign languages, environmental science, technical training for certain jobs, and preparation for the American Citizenship Test. You do not need to have a Bachelor's degree to be admitted. Courses start at about $100.

RAP (The Smithsonian Institution Resident Associate Program)

The programs listed below vary from evening lectures to 8-week courses on cultural subjects, such as:

- science, literature, music, art, architecture, and history
- study tours for adults to places, events, or exhibits in or near the Washington area.
- studio art courses on photography, painting, drawing, sculpture, ceramics, calligraphy, jewelry design, and other arts.

Fees start at $8. Tuition for 8-week courses is $70-$125 for members, $90-$160 for non-members. Membership costs $45-$55.

The Kennedy Center

The Kennedy Center Performance Plus Program has courses, lectures, and workshops on the performing arts—for example, ballet, opera, theater, and modern dance. Famous performers and directors often speak to the classes.

Courses cost from $6 for single classes to $150 for dinner-lecture series. Some events are free.

The National Geographic Society

Every Tuesday, the National Geographic Society has a lunchtime lecture and film series. At other times, the Society has music and dance performances, storytelling, and lectures on international topics.

Tuesday lunchtime series are free. Single classes start at $6; course series start at $15.

FONZ (Friends of the National Zoo)

The National Zoo has lectures, classes, and workshops on nature-related subjects—for example, nature photography, zoology, and veterinary studies. Some special programs are for families with children. A few programs are open only to FONZ members.

Memberships are $34 for individuals and $39 for a couple. Members get discounts on events and classes. Non-member fees start at $7.

Religious programs

Churches, synagogues, mosques, and other religious organizations offer classes on religious topics.

Learning Through Television

Some colleges have classes on cable TV—for example, on business, the humanities, history, and philosophy. To sign up, call the college and ask how to register. You can study these subjects at:

- many community colleges.
- the University of Maryland—through its University College program.

To complete a course, you will do homework and take a test at the end of the semester. Sometimes you can take the test at home and mail it to the school or college; at other times, you will take the test at the college.

You can also take some classes by renting or borrowing videotapes from the school or college. Call the admissions department of each college for information on how to join (see "Information").

The costs range from $200-$700 for classes on tape or on television.

Information

College testing information

Educational Testing Service.

- The TOEFL. TOEFL Office, P.O. Box 6151, Princeton, NJ 08541. 609/951-1100

- SAT, GRE, LSAT, MCAT exams. College Board, ATP, Department E-26, P.O. Box 6212, Princeton, NJ 08541. 609/951-1100

Miller Analogies Test Psychological Corporation, 7500 Oak Blvd., Cleveland, OH 44130.

Two-year community colleges

Montgomery College.

- Rockville: 301/279-5044
- Germantown: 301/353-7818
- Takoma Park: 301/650-1500

Prince George's Community College: 301/322-0866

Northern Virginia Community College (NOVA).

- Alexandria: 703/845-6200
- Annandale: 703/323-3000
- Manassas: 703/257-6600
- Sterling: 703/450-2501
- Woodbridge: 703/323-3000

Four-year colleges (off-campus programs)

The Johns Hopkins University: 301/294-7040

University of Virginia: 703/876-6900

University of Maryland University College: 301/985-7000

Public school continuing education

DC (Adult Education and Community Education Branch): 202/724-4209

MD

- Montgomery County Public Schools Adult Education. Montgomery County has a brochure listing the courses, times, and costs. If you are a county resident, get this brochure at the library or ask for one to be mailed to you. 301/929-2025
- Prince George's County Public Schools Adult Education: 301/386-1512

VA

- Alexandria City Public Schools, Community Education: 703/824-6845
- Arlington County Public Schools, Adult Education Department: 703/358-6900
- Fairfax County Public Schools Adult Education: 703/506-2200 or 703/506-2340

Public recreation departments

DC: 202/673-7660

MD

- Montgomery County: 301/217-6880
- City of Rockville: 301/424-8000, ext. 308
- Prince George's County: 301/699-2407

VA

- Arlington County: 703/358-6900
- Fairfax County: 703/506-2200 or 703/506-2340
- Falls Church: 703/241-5077

Enrichment programs.

- Corcoran School of Art: 202/628-9484
- Cultural Alliance of Greater Washington: 202/638-2406
- Foundation for Advanced Education in the Sciences (FAES): 301/496-5273 for a course catalog, or 301/496-7976 for general information.
- Friends of the National Zoo (FONZ): 202/673-4955
- The Kennedy Center Performance Plus Program: 202/416-8811
- The National Geographic Society: 202/857-7700
- The Smithsonian Institution Resident Associate Program (RAP): 202/357-3030
- USDA Graduate Program: 202/720-5885

Words to Know

Accredited: approved by the government; meeting certain standards

Admissions: applying to a school or college; doing all the necessary procedures to be admitted—such as filling out the application, having an interview, and taking the SAT

Advisor: a special member of the faculty (college staff) who helps students plan their academic programs

Assistantship: financial aid for a graduate student

Associate's degree: a degree offered at 2-year colleges

Audit: to take a course without receiving a grade or credit

Bachelor's degree: a degree you get for finishing a 4-year program

Brochure: a small book that gives details of a special program or event

College: a place for undergraduate study

Community college: a public, 2-year college

Credit hour: a unit of study earned by a student

Deadline: a specified date or time when you must complete or submit something; also called a "due date"

Degree: an award for finishing college—for example, Bachelor's, Master's, or Doctorate

Doctorate: the highest degree awarded by a university for advanced graduate research and study

Enrichment programs: non-degree, non-credit course programs on subjects such as art, literature, cooking, and sports

Exhibit: a showing or demonstration —usually of art or special objects

Fellowship: an award of financial aid, usually given to a graduate student on the basis of merit, need, and/or experience

Full-time: a student taking 12 or more credits per semester

Grade point average (GPA): The average of grade points earned for all completed courses. Usually, A=4 points; B=3 points; C=2 points. For example, a student who has two A's and one B has a GPA of 3.7 (4+4+3 divided by 3).

Grant: financial aid given to an undergraduate or graduate student—usually awarded to those who need the money

Higher education: post-secondary (after high school) education

Lecture: a speech made by a professor or expert in a particular subject

Master's degree (M.A., M.B.A., M.S., etc.): the first graduate degree awarded after completion of a Bachelor's degree. Usually, you study 1-3 years.

Professional school: an institution for the study of business, medicine, law, or other professional areas

Scholarship: a kind of educational financial assistance awarded to an undergraduate or graduate student

Semester: a period of study lasting about 14-16 weeks. Most colleges have two semesters (fall and spring) and a short summer semester.

Transcript: an official copy of your school record—including the courses you took and your grades

Tuition: the cost of a course

Two-year college: a college where you can get an Associate's degree

Undergraduate: a student who is completing an Associate's or

Bachelor's degree. You need an undergraduate degree for admission to a graduate program.

University: a place for undergraduate and graduate study

Workshop: an educational meeting, usually for a day or less

COLLEGE
BOUND   *Opening the Doors to Higher Education*

Shirley Levin, M.A.
College and Career Counselor

Help with choosing and applying to college

Experience placing international students in colleges in USA

Group presentations on request

Telephone or write: College Bound
6809 Breezewood Terrace
Rockville, Maryland 20852
Telephone: 301-468-6668

Staying Informed

Major Newspapers

Local

The Washington Post	1-800/477-4679
The Washington Times	202/636-3333
The Washington Business Journal	
	703/875-2205 or 703/816-0315

National

USA Today	1-800/872-0001
The Wall Street Journal	301/622-2900

Magazines

Local

Washingtonian	202/331-0715

National

Time	1-800/843-8463
Newsweek	1-800/631-1040
People	1-800/541-9000

Television News

	Channel	Network
WRC	4	NBC
WTTG	5	FOX
WJLA	7	ABC
WUSA	9	CBS
WETA	26	PBS
Cable	varies	CNN
Cable	varies	C-SPAN
Cable	varies	Headline News
Cable	varies	Newschannel 8
Cable	varies	CNBC
Cable	varies	The Weather Channel

Radio News

	Station
WMAL	630 AM
WTOP	1500 AM
WAMU	88.5 FM

Periodicals

Newspapers

The two most popular daily newspapers, or dailies, are *The Washington Post* and *The Washington Times* (see this chapter's opener). Both the *Post* and the *Times* have international, national, and local news.

 At the newsstand, the *Post* and the *Times* cost 25¢ on Mondays through Saturdays. On Sundays, the price is $1.50 for the *Post* and 75¢ for the *Times*. For home delivery, you pay $2.30 per week for the *Post* and $13 per 3-month period for the *Times*. Tax may be added to the price of delivery.

Other popular dailies. The most popular daily newspapers printed outside the Washington area are:

- *The New York Times* (general news).
- *The Wall Street Journal* (business).
- *USA Today* (a popular, easy-to-read newspaper that goes all over the country).

Community. Newspapers give the news about a local area—for example, what stores are having sales, what movies are playing nearby, and what jobs are open.

Most community newspapers are published weekly—for example, the *Gazette* and the *Journal*. Many are delivered to your home for free. If not, you can get them at small food stores in your area.

Ethnic. The Washington area has several foreign language and ethnic newspapers. Some are published daily—for example, the *Korean Times*; others are published weekly—for example, the *Washington Jewish Week*.

Out-of-town and international. You can get these at a few newsstands and bookstores or through the mail. International newspapers cost 75¢-$3 a copy.

You can get many of these newspapers on the day of publication, but others (especially international ones) may be 2-3 days late. Newspapers delivered through the mail often arrive weeks after publication.

Magazines

Local. The largest local magazine is the *Washingtonian*, which has many hints about shopping, dining, and

Newspapers and magazines are cheaper if you subscribe rather than buy regularly from the newsstands. To subscribe, buy one copy of the magazine from a newsstand. Usually, the magazine will have a subscription card. If not, look for the address and send a postcard asking for information.

entertainment; it also has stories about successful people in Washington.

National. The most popular news magazines are:

- *Time.*
- *Newsweek.*

People magazine has stories about the lives and loves of famous people; it is easier to read than news magazines.

Bookstores

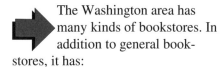

The Washington area has many kinds of bookstores. In addition to general bookstores, it has:

- used bookstores.
- specialty bookstores with books on subjects such as religion, art, or cooking.
- museum bookstores with games, calendars, tapes, and even jewelry.

Discounts. Many bookstores give discounts for books that are on the "best seller" list. Also look for bookstores that sell only at a discount—they are in most shopping malls.

Paying. Take the book to the cashier. Most bookstores take cash, checks, and credit cards.

Returning. Some bookstores let you return books, but you must return them before a certain date. Ask the salesperson about the store's policy.

Libraries

Public libraries

Public libraries are free. In addition to books and magazines, libraries often have:

- music on records, audio cassette tapes, and compact discs.
- video tapes.
- newsletters about topics such as job openings, babysitting, and adult education.
- foreign language books, magazines, and newspapers. Ask which library in your county or city has the language you want.
- reference books—such as encyclopedias and directories in the reference section. You cannot borrow these books, but you can look at them in the library.
- activities—such as adult education courses and storytelling sessions for children.

To borrow (take out) books, you need a library card. You can get a card at the information desk if you show proof of residence—for example, a utility bill or copy of your lease.

How to borrow a book

1. **Find the nearest library.**

Look up the list of numbers for your county or for DC in the blue pages of your phone book; call any library and ask which one is closest to your home.

2. Find the books you want to borrow.

A librarian at the information desk will show you how to find the books.

3. Go to the checkout counter.

Tell the librarian you want a library card; show your proof of residence and get a card. Each member of your family can get a separate library card.

4. Ask for a list of the library's rules.

Find out:

- how many books or tapes you can take out.
- how long you can keep these books and tapes—usually 2-3 weeks for books and 1-7 days for a tape.
- how much you have to pay if you do not return the books on time—about 5¢-20¢ per day per book (Sundays and holidays do not count).
- what the hours are.

5. Give the librarian the items you want to borrow.

The librarian will stamp the due date on each item.

6. Return the books and tapes before or on the due date.

You can return your books to any library branch within the same county. If the library is open, look for the "Return Books" sign; if the library is closed, look for a "Book Drop" slot on the outside wall.

What if I want to keep the book past the due date? Bring the book to the library and tell them you want to renew it. If you cannot get to the library in time, call and ask if you can renew your book(s) without bringing them in.

Special libraries

College libraries. All area universities and colleges have their own libraries. Most private colleges will let you look at the books, but you cannot borrow them unless you are a student or faculty member. Some public college libraries—such as Montgomery College—let all residents of the county borrow books.

Library of Congress. This is the largest library in the country. You need a photo ID card—for example, a driver's license or passport—to use the library.

Radio

AM/FM. Your radio has two settings:

- AM. Most AM stations have news and sports broadcasts, as well as some music stations.
- FM. Stations on this setting are clearer than most AM stations. Most music stations are on FM.

Stations. Most radio stations are local —you cannot get them outside of the Washington area. See this chapter's opener for some of the most popular stations. Other popular stations are:

- WJZE FM (100.3) for jazz.
- WMAL AM (630) for news, talk shows, and sports.
- WPGC FM (95.5) for rock.

Public radio. National Public Radio (NPR) has classical music and information programs—such as news, interviews, and special reports. The two Washington NPR stations are:

- WAMU FM (88.5).
- WETA FM (90.9).

Television (TV)

Network television

These stations are free on any television. In some places, the picture and sound are clear; in others, they are not. If you are having trouble, install an antenna or get cable television.

Major television stations.

- NBC (Channel 4).
- Fox Television (Channel 5).
- ABC (Channel 7).
- CBS (Channel 9).

Public stations.

Public stations have films and cultural programs. The local public stations are:

- Maryland Public Television (Channel 22).
- WETA (Channel 26).
- WHMM (Channel 32).

Cable television

This is a paid service that gives you:

- more stations or channels.
- better reception on all channels.

Programs. Cable programs include:

- films.
- sports events.
- concerts.
- foreign language stations.
- local, national, and international news.
- educational programs.
- family programs.

Installation. You may get cable TV in most areas. If you live in an apartment building, first ask the building manager if the building is wired for cable TV.

To have cable TV installed in your home, call the cable company for your area (see "Information"). Ask the company for:

- booklets that explain what each cable channel has.
- a sample cable guide.
- the cost (see below).

The cost is different for each company. Make sure you get a list of the prices for each service; also ask about discounts or "specials."

Some items are a one-time charge and some are monthly:

- installation: $30-$60.
- converter box: sometimes a $20-$25 deposit; sometimes you pay a monthly fee.
- remote control: sometimes a monthly fee; sometimes free.
- rebroadcast (main local and national channels): about $14 a month.
- basic cable channels (about 50 channels): about $25-$35 a month.
- premium channels (about seven to eight channels): $10-$15 a month per channel.

You can find out more about cable TV programs by looking at:

- the special channels on your TV that give program schedules.
- a cable guide—a magazine with all the cable listings. It costs about $1 a month.
- the weekly TV guide in your newspaper or at your local supermarket.

Videos

Renting

You can go to a video store to rent videos to watch at home. Most stores have movies (including foreign films), documentary films, exercise pro-

grams, and concerts. Some video stores specialize in foreign films.

 You may pay a membership fee in some smaller stores. The nightly rental cost is:

- $1-$3; newer films may cost about $1 more.
- $4-$10 for a video machine (VCR)—with a deposit.

 If you don't return the video tape on time, you must pay a "late fee" of $1-$2 per day. Most video stores have a return box outside the store for returning video-tapes when the store is closed.

Buying

You may buy videos at most video rental stores and at book and record stores.

 Some popular videos cost under $10, but most videotapes cost about $20-$40.

Conversions

Foreign-made TV sets

You may be able to use the TV set from your home country. Ask at an electronics company that specializes in international video to help you choose the attachments or adapters you need.

 Find out what you need for your TV set or any other electronic equipment before you plug it in. Otherwise, you may damage your equipment.

Foreign-made videos

Most foreign-made video cassette tapes cannot be used on American VCRs. You can convert:

- foreign-made cassettes for American machines.
- American-made cassettes for foreign machines.

To have a video converted, call a video production service. The price of converting a 2-hour video is about $45-$55.

Information

Libraries

DC: 202/727-1126

MD

- Montgomery County: 301/217-4636
- Prince George's County: 301/699-3500

VA

- Alexandria: 703/858-4558
- Arlington County: 703/358-5990
- Fairfax County: 703/222-3155
- Falls Church: 703/538-3838

Cable TV

DC

- District Cablevision: 202/332-8777

MD

- Montgomery County
  - Montgomery Cable TV: 301/424-4400

- Prince George's County.
  - Multivision Cable TV: 301/731-4260 or 937-3760
  - Metrovision Cable TV: 301/499-2930

VA

- Alexandria: 703/823-3000
- Arlington: 703/841-7700
- Fairfax County: 703/378-8411

Words to Know

Cable television: a paid TV service. You get extra channels and better reception on your TV.

Conversion: changing something (a video cassette or a machine)

Dailies: newspapers published every day

Home delivery: a service that brings, the newspaper to your door

Network TV: the free TV stations

Premium channels: cable TV channels that show movies and sports

Subscribe: to pay for a newspaper or magazine to be delivered regularly to you

Bookstores

The Book Cellar. 8227 Woodmont Ave., Bethesda, MD 20814. 301/654-1898. Used & rare books. All topics, languages. Open 7 days.

Making the Life That's Saved Worth Living

Each year, the lives of thousands of people are saved by advances in medical knowledge and technology. Many of those who are saved are permanently disabled. They can't walk, talk, drive, or even get around in their own homes.

At the National Rehabilitation Hospital in northwest Washington, D.C., we help people learn to help themselves. Through specialized medical care, therapy and other services, we focus on abilities rather than *dis*abilities. Our goal is to enable people to be as active and independent as possible.

At NRH—one of the top medical rehabilitation hospitals in the nation—we offer inpatient and outpatient services for adults and adolescents with disabilities from stroke, head or spinal cord injury, amputation, arthritis, chronic pain, post-polio syndrome, multiple sclerosis, and other conditions.

To find out more, contact the NRH Admissions Office, 102 Irving St., NW, Washington, DC 20010-2949; (202) 877-1152.

National Rehabilitation Hospital

102 Irving Street, NW
Washington, DC 20010. 2949

A not-for-profit member of **MEDLANTIC** Healthcare Group ®

Medical Care

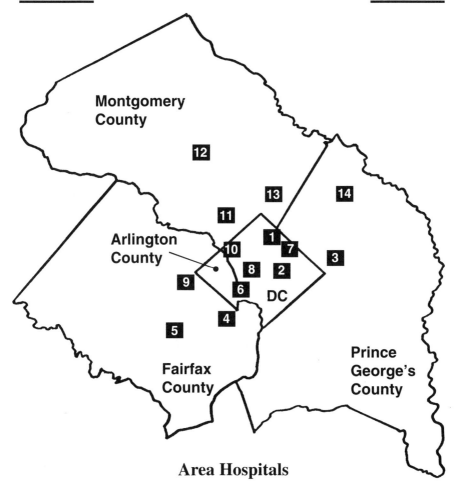

Area Hospitals

1. **Washington Hospital Center:** *202/877-7000*
   Children's Hospital: *202/745-5000*

2. **Howard University:** *202/865-6100*

3. **Prince George's:** *301/774-8882*

4. **Alexandria:** *703/379-3000*

5. **Fairfax:** *703/698-1110*

6. **George Washington University:** *202/994-1000*

7. **National Rehabilitation** *202/877-1000*

8. **Georgetown University:** *202/784-2000*

9. **Arlington:** *703/558-5000*

10. **Sibley Memorial:** *202/537-4111*

11. **Suburban:** *301/530-3100*

12. **Shady Grove:** *301/279-868-8000*

13. **Holy Cross:** *301/905-0100*

14. **Laurel-Beltsville:** *301/725-4300*

__Medicine Labels__

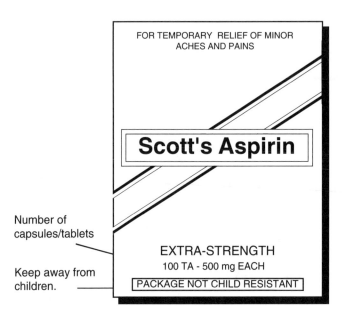

FOR TEMPORARY RELIEF OF MINOR
ACHES AND PAINS

Scott's Aspirin

Over the Counter

no doctor's order needed

Number of
capsules/tablets

EXTRA-STRENGTH
100 TA - 500 mg EACH

Keep away from
children.

PACKAGE NOT CHILD RESISTANT

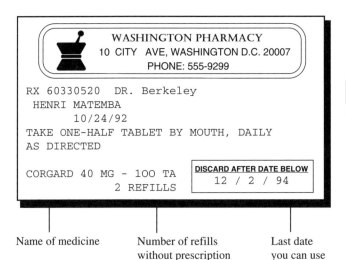

WASHINGTON PHARMACY
10 CITY AVE, WASHINGTON D.C. 20007
PHONE: 555-9299

RX 60330520   DR. Berkeley
 HENRI MATEMBA
      10/24/92
TAKE ONE-HALF TABLET BY MOUTH, DAILY
AS DIRECTED

CORGARD 40 MG - 1OO TA
         2 REFILLS

DISCARD AFTER DATE BELOW
12 / 2 / 94

Prescription

doctor's order needed

Name of medicine

Number of refills
without prescription

Last date
you can use

Doctors/ Dentists

Physicians (doctors)

Family doctors (also called general practitioners or primary-care physicians) give general medical care.

Specialists have special training for certain types of medicine. Some serve as primary-care physicians and can take care of your general medical needs—for example:

- pediatricians for children.
- gynecologists and obstetricians for women.
- internists for internal medicine.

The average cost for a first visit to a doctor is $75-$100. Often, you also pay fees for lab tests and X-rays. The amount you pay depends on the type of insurance you have (see "Insurance").

Dentists

Find a general-care, family dentist for basic dental care. Some dentists specialize in working with children.

You may want to get a written cost estimate for expensive treatments. (There may be a small charge for the estimate.) Sample costs are:

- Routine exam (cleaning and two X-rays): $70-$125 (10%-20% less for children).
- Filling: $75-$140.

If you visit the dentist often and have a lot of treatments, you may save money with a prepaid dental plan or dental insurance (see "Insurance"). The disadvantages of prepaid plans are:

- You must use a dentist who works with the plan.
- The dentist may not spend as much time per visit as a private dentist would.

Finding a Professional

Most hospitals and some doctors' offices have interpreters in several languages. Call your local hospital and ask if interpreters are available in your language. This service is free.

Bring all medical documents from your home country to the U.S. Have the documents translated and notarized. You will need copies for your doctors and for your insurance company.

Where to look

To find a doctor or dentist, ask:

- your health insurance company. Often, you must use a doctor or dentist listed with the insurance company.
- an association for dentists or doctors (see "Information").

What to look for

Group or individual practice. If the doctor or dentist shares the office with other doctors, can you see the same doctor or dentist every time you visit?

Hospital. To which hospital(s) does the doctor or dentist admit patients? Is this the hospital you want?

Insurance. Will the doctor or dentist wait for the insurance money? Or must you pay the whole bill and then get the money yourself (see "Insurance")?

Your Visit

For your first visit to the doctor or dentist, you need a check or a credit card to pay the bill, in case the office does not accept insurance as payment.

You will also need:

- medical records such as
  - medical or dental history.
  - immunization history.
  - dental X-rays.
- names or prescriptions of medicines you need.

- insurance forms for your doctor or dentist to sign.
- a check or a credit card to pay the bill, in case the office does not accept insurance as payment.

How to visit the doctor or dentist

1. **Make an appointment.**

Call your doctor or dentist's office as soon as possible—you may have to wait several days or even weeks.

2. **Complete the forms you get at the office.**

If you have any questions, ask the receptionist.

3. **Pay for the visit.**

Pay at the reception desk after you see the doctor or dentist. If the office files the insurance claim for you, then you have to pay for only your part of the bill (see "Insurance").

4. **Schedule your next appointment if necessary.**

5. **Get any medication you need at a pharmacy.**

6. **File your insurance claim.**

Mail this claim with a copy of the doctor or dentist's bill. This is not necessary if the doctor or dentist has filed the claim for you.

Eyeglasses/ Contacts

Who can help

Ophthalmologists are trained physicians or medical doctors. Opthalmologists mainly do eye surgery and treat eye diseases. Most also prescribe lenses for eyeglasses; a few fit contact lenses.

Optometrists are trained eye specialists. They mainly prescribe lenses for eyeglasses and fit contact lenses.

Optical shops

Many optometrists work in optical shops (eye centers). When you go to the shop, you can get an exam and pick out your frames. Sometimes you may get the glasses in an hour; if you have a special type of lens, you may have to wait a week or more.

 Most optical shops are open 6 days a week, from about 9 am-6 or 7 pm. Often, you do not need an appointment. Call ahead for an optometrist in a private office or for an ophthalmologist.

 Optometrists charge $35 or more for the exam. Ophthalmologists usually cost more. Other costs are about:

- $80-$300 for contact lenses, depending on the type of lens.
- $60 or more for eyeglass lenses.
- $50-$200 and more for eyeglass frames.

Medicine

Choose a pharmacy that is close to your home or office and is open 24 hours a day. The pharmacy will keep records of your medications.

 Read the label on all medicine packages for instructions. Look for warnings—such as "Take with food" or "May cause drowsiness." If you have small children, look for "child-safety caps."

Overview

Over-the-counter or non-prescription drugs. These are for minor problems—such as common colds, headaches, and allergies. You can get these drugs at most pharmacies, supermarkets, groceries, and convenience stores.

Prescription drugs. Common prescription drugs are antibiotics, codeine, and birth control pills. You will need a prescription from your doctor.

 Prices for over-the-counter medicines range from $3 for a small bottle of aspirin to $50 for arthritis cream. Most common prescriptions cost $20-$40 (for most antibiotics), but some medicines can cost much more.

Some insurance plans pay for prescription drugs—but not over-the-counter drugs (see "Insurance").

Ask your pharmacist or doctor if you can buy a generic drug (one that does not use the manufacturer's brand name); generic drugs cost 10%-75% less.

How to get prescription drugs

1. **Call the doctor.**

Have the number of your pharmacy ready in case the doctor wants to call and order the medicine (see below).

2. **Visit the doctor if necessary.**

You will get the prescription after your examination.

3. **Take the prescription to your pharmacy.**

If your health insurance pays for drugs, bring your insurance card.

4. **Get a refill.**

Many prescriptions can be refilled; that is, you do not need another prescription for the same medicine. The number of times you can get a refill is on the label.

If your medicine can be refilled, call the pharmacy ahead of time. Give the "Rx" number on the label.

Note: Sometimes, you do not have to visit the doctor; he or she will call the pharmacy and order the prescription. Wait a while and then call the pharmacy; make sure the

prescription is ready before you go to pick it up.

Hospitals

Overview

There are two types of hospitals: public and private. Public hospitals are usually run by a local government and do not make a profit. Private hospitals are run by corporations or charitable organizations.

Public hospitals are generally less expensive than private hospitals. In general, you will pay about $1,000 a night for a hospital stay. This cost includes lab tests—but not doctor's fees.

Emergency care is expensive. You pay for:

- the emergency room: $100-$130.
- the physician's fee: about $50-$200 per hour.
- any medication you get.

Other possible fees are for surgery, X-rays, and lab tests. Your health insurance will pay at least part of these costs.

What to look for

Type and quality of services. Most hospitals treat all kinds of problems, but some specialize in certain medical areas—such as cardiology.

Connection with a university. Some of the best hospitals are at teaching/research medical facilities.

Facilities. Some hospitals have flexible visiting hours. If you have a special diet, ask about the food.

Getting to the hospital

In an emergency.

Call **911** for an ambulance or go to the nearest hospital. Keep the name, number, and address of at least one hospital in a place where you can find it easily (see "In an Emergency" at the beginning of this book).

 Ask your insurance company what to do in an emergency, both in the area and out of town. If you do not follow the correct procedures, the company may not pay for the services you get.

Non-emergency service.

Your doctor will refer you to a hospital for non-emergency service when you need special lab tests, extensive medical treatment, or surgery.

Insurance

Overview

You can get group insurance for yourself and your family through an organization—such as:

- your employer.

- your university (if you are a student or professor).
- some professional associations (if you are a member).

Individual plans. You can get insurance for yourself and your family on an individual plan directly from:

- an insurance company.
- a Health Maintenance Organization (see "HMOs").

Only a few insurance companies give individual coverage if you do not have a green card or if you are not a U.S. citizen. Get group insurance if you can.

 Health insurance costs vary. An individual (non-group) plan might cost $250-$500 a month for one person. An individual family plan can cost $500-$1,000 for a family with two children. Group plans cost much less.

The cost of health insurance depends on:

- the type of plan.
- the kind of coverage, or what it pays for.
- your gender (male or female).
- your age.
- your physical condition.

What it pays for

Insurance coverage varies. Some insurance plans pay for:

- visits to the doctor for illnesses and injuries (not routine visits).
- maternity care.

211

- emergency care.
- hospitalization.
- prescription drugs.
- eyeglasses.

Sometimes, you can get dental insurance as part of your plan. (Individual dental insurance is hard to get.) Dental insurance may help pay for:

- routine care (cleanings, X-rays).
- emergency care.
- oral surgery.
- orthodontic care (for making the teeth straight).

What to look for

Doctors and dentists. Who are the primary-care doctors and dentists and participating specialists?

Hospitals. Which hospitals must you use?

Coverage.

- What medical services and conditions are covered?
- Does the insurance pay for out-of-area coverage or for emergency care in a hospital that is not part of the plan?

Limitations.

- What medical services or conditions are not covered?
- What exceptions or restrictions apply?

Cost. Ask about the following fees:

- premium. The monthly, quarterly (every 3 months), or annual fee.

- co-payment. The percentage of the bill you pay when you receive medical services. Usually, this is about 20%.
- deductible. An amount of money the insurance does not pay. For example, if you have a $250 deductible, you pay $250 toward your medical bills. The insurance company pays for most of the expenses over this $250.
- ceiling. The most money an insurance company will pay during a specific period of time.

HMOs

Overview

Many people use an HMO (Health Maintenance Organization) instead of insurance. With an HMO, you choose a primary-care physician from a list of the HMO's doctors or dentists.

The advantages of an HMO are:

- It often costs much less than a traditional insurance plan.
- You do not have to file claims.

The disadvantages are:

- You must use a doctor, dentist, or hospital that works with the HMO.
- You might not always be able to see the same doctor or dentist when you visit.
- The doctor or dentist may have a lot of patients and be unable to spend much time with you.

For a set monthly, quarterly, semi-annual (two times a year), or annual fee, you can see your HMO doctor or dentist as often as you want; you pay a small fee ($5-$10) for each visit. Annual premiums can range from $710 for a single person with a group plan, to $2,500 for a single person with an individual plan.

Abbreviations

ACU: Acupuncture
CD: Cardiovascular diseases
DDS: Dentistry
D: Dermatology
GP: General practice
GER: Geriatrics
GYN: Gynecology
IM: Internal medicine
OBS: Obstetrics
OBG: Obstetrics and gynecology
PD: Pediatrics

Information

Medical societies

DC

- American Medical Association: 202/789-7400
- Medical Society of the District of Columbia: 202/466-1800

MD

- Montgomery County Medical Society: 301/921-4300

- Prince George's County Medical Society: 301/341-7758

VA

- Alexandria Medical Society: 703/751-4611
- Arlington Medical Society: 703/528-0888
- Fairfax County Medical Society: 703/560-4855

Dental societies

- American Dental Association: 202/898-2400
- DC Dental Association: 202/547-7613
- Maryland Dental Association: 301/345-4196
- Virginia Dental Association: 703/642-5297

Words to Know

Cardiology: the treatment and study of heart disease

Ceiling: the highest amount insurance companies will pay for a medical service in one year

Co-payment: a small amount of money that you pay for each doctor or hospital visit. Your HMO pays the rest.

Cost estimate: the amount you will probably have to pay for a service

Deductible: an amount of money your insurance *does not* pay

213

Family doctor: a doctor that cares for families (also a "general practitioner")

Filling: the silver that the dentist puts in any holes in your teeth

General practitioner: a doctor that handles common medical problems

Generic drug: a drug that does not use a manufacturer's brand name

Group plan: an insurance plan you get as part of a group

Gynecologist: a doctor for women

HMO: Health Maintenance Organization; a kind of medical insurance

Individual plan: a plan you get by yourself—not as part of a group. You pay the full cost of your own medical insurance

Insurance claim: a form you send to your insurance company

Internist: a doctor of internal medicine

Lab test: a test of your blood, urine, or other body fluids

Maternity care: medical services for pregnant women

Obstetrician: a doctor for pregnant women

Ophthalmologist: a physician who specializes in eye care

Optometrist: a specialist in fitting and prescribing contact lenses and eyeglasses

Oral surgery: surgery of the mouth, teeth, gums, and jaw

Orthodontic care: dental services to straighten teeth

Over-the-counter drug: medicine that you can get without a prescription

Pediatrician: a doctor for children

Premium: an amount of money that you pay an insurance company for coverage

Prescription: a note from your doctor that allows you to get special medicine from a pharmacy

Private hospital: a non-government hospital

Public hospital: a hospital managed by the government

Refill: a prescription medicine that the pharmacy may fill again without permission from your doctor

X-ray: a photograph of the inside of your body

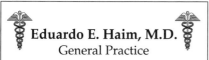
215

Need a Doctor?

Call CenterLine, **Washington Hospital Center's** physician referral line. We KNOW our doctors. We can answer your questions. We can give you directions. We can make your first appointment. We can even help find you doctors who speak your language.

Call us for a family physician or specialist in any of our medical or surgical departments, including our well respected centers of excellence:

- Washington Heart
- Washington National Eye Center
- The Cancer Institute
- Transplantation Services
- The Burn Center
- MEDSTAR/Shock-Trauma

WASHINGTON HOSPITAL CENTER
110 Irving Street, NW
Washington, DC 20010-2975

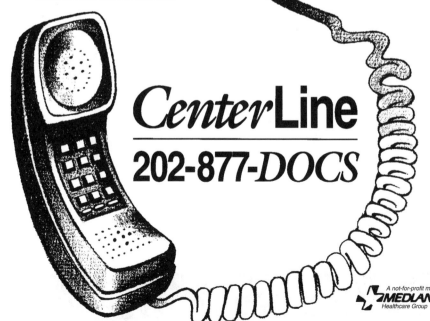

*Center*Line
202-877-DOCS

A not-for-profit member of
MEDLANTIC
Healthcare Group

HELLO! AMERICA BOOK ORDER FORM

NAME

STREET

CITY   STATE   ZIP CODE

COUNTRY   DAYTIME PHONE (   )

	QTY	PRICE	TOTAL
Hello! Washington		**$12.95**	
"Words to Know" in Spanish (available in September) Términos útiles aparacerá en español (a partir de Septièmbre)		**$4.95**	
Add 5% sales tax (for Maryland address only)			
Shipping & Handling (choose one)			

Domestic	REGULAR (2-7 days)	$2.00; 75¢ each additional book	
	RUSH (1 day)	$4.00; 75¢ each additional book	
Canada	REGULAR (8-20 days)	$5.00 per book	
	RUSH (7 days)	$7.50 per book	
International	REGULAR (8-20 days)	$7.00 per book	
	RUSH (7 days)	$10.00 per book	

Total Amount Due

Payment. Call for shipping costs on bulk orders.
Make checks payable to Hello! America, Inc.
- Individuals: Orders must be prepaid, using personal checks, VISA or MasterCard.
- Individuals from outside the U.S.: Payment must be in U.S. dollars with 1) check with MICR-encoding drawn on a U.S. bank, 2) international postal money order, or 3) VISA or MasterCard.

VISA   **MasterCard**   Expiration Date

VISA or MasterCard Number

Signature

Print Cardholder's Name

☐ I want information on Personal Orientation Services.

MAIL! Hello! America, 7701 Woodmont Ave., #1108, Bethesda, MD 20814

PHONE! 301-913-0074   **FAX!** 301/652-4566

218

Looking and ___Feeling Good___

D.C.
District of Columbia 202/767-7345
- Archery
- Basketball
- Softball
- Volleyball

Maryland
Montgomery County 301/217-6790
- Basketball
- Flag Football
- Soccer
- Softball
- Tennis
- Volleyball

Prince George's County 301/699-2400
- Basketball
- Floor Hockey
- Softball
- Touch Football
- Volleyball

Virginia
Arlington County 703/358-4710
- Basketball
- Flag Football
- Soccer
- Softball
- Tennis
- Volleyball

Alexandria 703/838-4345
- Basketball
- Softball
- Soccer
- Volleyball

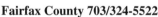

Fairfax County 703/324-5522
- Baseball
- Basketball
- Flag Football
- Soccer
- Softball
- Tennis
- Volleyball
- Touch Football
- Lacrosse
- Running

Outdoor Fun

Parks and paths

Rock Creek Park is the largest park in the area. It goes from the Potomac River in northwest Washington to Olney, MD. The park has over 2,100 acres in the District and over 4,400 acres in Montgomery County.

You cannot camp in the park, but you can:

- jog or hike.
- ride a bicycle or a horse.
- picnic.
- play tennis (at Pierce Mill).
- see art exhibits (at the Art Barn).
- watch birds and other wildlife.
- visit the Nature Center and a planetarium.

To get there: Many roads and smaller streets go into the park. To reach the Information Center, go north on 16th St., NW, and turn left on Military Road. Follow the signs to the park.

The Mall, Ellipse, and Tidal Basin are close together in downtown Washington. Many people jog here, especially during lunch hour. In the spring and summer, many people rent paddleboats at the Tidal Basin.

The Chesapeake & Ohio (C&O) Canal starts in Georgetown and goes 184 miles west to Cumberland, MD. The paths are especially popular on the weekends. In addition to jogging and riding a bicycle, you may rent rowboats for about $15 an hour at:

- Thompson's Boat House.
- Fletcher's Boat House.
- Swain's Lock Boat House.

To get there: The towpath has many entrances along Canal Road in northwest Washington and Cabin John, MD. In Georgetown, you can walk there anywhere from 29th to 33rd streets, between M and K streets.

Great Falls Park in Virginia has beautiful scenery—with rock formations, forests, swamps, and all kinds of animal life. Some of its paths go beside the Potomac River. There is a small entrance fee.

To get there: Take VA 193 northwest from Exit 13 of the Beltway to VA 738 (Old Dominion Dr.). Turn right at the park entrance.

The National Arboretum has 444 acres of:

- rolling hills with different kinds of trees—including a bonsai exhibit.

This chapter's opener has a list of sports activities run by your local government. The "Information" section has a list of numbers for the major parks and a list of sports clubs and leagues.

- gardens—including rose, azalea, and Japanese gardens. The gardens change with the seasons.

To get there: Go east on New York Ave. The sign for the visitors entrance is about half a block past Bladensburg Rd., NE.

Kenilworth Aquatic Gardens has 12 acres of ponds filled with unusual water plants. In fact, these ponds have over 100,000 different types of plants—including tropical waterlilies and Egyptian lotuses. The park around the gardens has 44 acres of wet lands, or marshes. Picnic tables are available.

To get there: Go east on New York Ave. After you cross the Anacostia River, turn south on Kenilworth Ave., right on Douglas St., NE, and right on Anacostia Ave., NE. The parking lot is on the left.

Sports

Golfing

Public courses. To find out about a public course near you, call the parks department in your area. Some courses takes reservations.

Private clubs require an initiation fee and annual dues. You also must be sponsored by two people who are already members.

 Public courses usually cost about $9 a person for nine holes, or $18 a person for 18 holes.

Private clubs may cost up to $30,000 for the initiation fee; $1,200-$2,000 annual dues.

Tennis

There are many tennis courts in the Washington area; a few are indoors—such as those at Hains Point in the District and Cabin John and Wheaton Regional Parks in Montgomery County, MD (see "Information").

 Some courts are free, but you may need to call first and reserve a court or get there early. Courts may have either hard or soft surfaces; they cost from $8-$16 per hour, depending on the time of day and the time of year. Indoor courts cost more.

Health Clubs

What to look for

Programs and equipment. Make sure the club has the kind of program or equipment you want.

Location. Find a club that is near your home or office.

Certification. The staff members should have degrees or special training in physical education.

Child care. Many clubs have babysitters.

The contract

To join a health club, you will sign a contract. Read the terms carefully;

have someone translate for you if you do not know English very well.

Initiation fees are from $25 (YWCA) to $1,500 (Four Seasons Fitness Club). Monthly charges range from $15-$96. If you pay the whole fee when you sign up, you may save some money.

If you sign a 2-year contract, you will have to keep paying, even if you move out of the area. Most clubs will give you a 6-month contract if you ask.

What if I change my mind after I sign the contract? You may cancel if you tell the club within 3 days.

Massages/ Spas

Where to go

You can get a massage:

- in a fitness center. Many fitness centers have massages, saunas, and steam baths.
- in a full-service beauty salon or day spa. You can spend from 45 minutes to a full day there.
- from a massage practitioner.

What to look for

Qualifications. A practitioner or center should be licensed or accredited.

Services. Call up and ask what type of massage you will get. If the person on the phone will not tell you, do not go; many "massage parlors" have illegal activities.

Generally, massages cost about $40 an hour, but some massages may cost $65 an hour or more. If you ask a practitioner to come to you, the cost may be more than $100 an hour.

You do not have to tip if you get a massage in the practitioner's office; give a 10%-20% tip if the practitioner comes to you.

Beauty Salons

Hair

Many "quick" salons do not require an appointment, but you need to make an appointment at some of the better salons. Most salons are open from 10am-5pm, Monday Saturday. A few are open 7 days a week.

Tipping: In general, tip about 15% of the total bill. If the person who serves you owns the salon, some Americans do not tip; decide for yourself. In a hair salon, the shampoo girl usually gets about $1.

You can get a haircut at many quick, unisex (for both men and women) salons for around $10. Many salons charge about $35; a few charge as much as $65. Full-head hair coloring prices range from $35–$65.

Nails

Beauty salons give manicures for $12–$14.

Salons that specialize in nail care offer additional treatments. One of the most popular is an acrylic treatment that hardens nails and helps them stay pretty longer. Acrylic treatments are usually $60–$70.

Information

Parks and paths

Cabin John Regional Park: 301/299-1990

Great Falls Park: 703/285-2966

Kenilworth Aquatic Gardens: 202/426-6905

National Arboretum: 202/475-4815

National Capital Region National Park Service. Information on renting boats and bicycles at Rock Creek Park, the Tidal Basin, or the C&O Canal. 202/619-7222 or 202/485-9666

National Park Service (NPS). Information on camping in the U.S. 202/208-4747

Rock Creek Park Horse Center: 202/362-0117

Thompson's Boat House—Bike Rentals and Boats: 202/333-9543

Wheaton Regional Park: 301/946-9071

Leagues

Sports Network. Tournaments and instruction, including soccer, volley-ball, and lacrosse. 703/631-5123

General outdoor clubs

American Youth Hostels (AYH). Outdoor events such as rafting, biking, canoeing, cross-country skiing. The club also gives you access to hostels all around the world. Open to all ages. 202/783-4944

Audubon Naturalist Society (ANS). Field trips, classes, workshops, lectures, and natural history tours. 301/652-9188

Potomac Appalachian Trail Club. Hiking, cross-country skiing, and rock climbing trips. 703/242-0965

Sierra Club. Has environmental activities and awareness and sponsors local outings. 202/547-5551

Washington Women Outdoors, Inc. Activities for women such as rock climbing and cross-country skiing. 301/864-3070

Bicycling

Potomac Peddlers Touring Club. The largest bicycling club in the Washington area. 202/363-TOUR (363-8687)

Golf

Rock Creek Golf Club. Plays on the 18-hole Rock Creek Course in northwest DC. The club will help you to find golfing partners. 202/462-3238 (days and weekends); 202/955-1549 (evenings). Ask for Priscilla McClain.

Hiking

Capital Hiking Club. Weekly Sunday trips to the Appalachian Trail. 703/578-1942

Center Hiking Club. Weekend trips to the mountains and the coast. 703/751-3971

Northern Virginia Hiking Club. Hikes in the George Washington National Forest and Shenandoahs. 703/491-4632. Ask for Bob Delmore.

Ice skating

Skating Club of Northern Virginia. 301/589-2063 (evenings and weekends). Ask for Debrah Weidman.

Suburban Skating Club. 301/805-0135. Ask for Dot Zucker.

Running

Road Runners Club of America. 703/836-0558

DC Road Runners Club. 703/241-0395

Montgomery County Road Runners Club. 301/353-0200

Skiing

Ski Club of Washington, DC. Plans ski events in the winter and other events in the off-season. 703/532-7776 or 703/536-8273

Ski conditions: 202/334-9000 ext. 4300

Soccer

United States Soccer Federation. Information about local leagues and about the 1994 World Cup. 201/861-6277

DC/Virginia Soccer Association. 703/321-7254 (mornings). Ask for Wallace Watson.

Maryland State Soccer Association. 1-410/744-5864. Ask for Anna Steffen.

Washington Area Women's Soccer. Top area women soccer players compete in the fall and spring. 703/827-7907

Tennis

Mid-Atlantic Tennis Association (MATA) / United States Tennis Association (USTA). Sponsors 150 tournaments throughout the year. Leagues for six ability levels. 703/560-9480

Volleyball

Mid-Atlantic Volleyball Association (MAV) and Federation of Outdoor Volleyball Associations (FOVA). 301/881-7795

Words to Know

Acrylic treatment: a treatment that makes fingernails strong

Beauty salon: a place that cuts your hair and treats your nails

Certification: meeting government standards

Contract: a written agreement between two people or a person and a company—such as a rental agreement, a bill of sale, or a club membership

Hair coloring: a treatment that changes the hair color

Health club: a place where you go to exercise

Initiation fee: money you pay to join a club

Massage practitioner: a person who gives massages

Softball: a kind of baseball. The ball is softer and larger.

Touch football: a kind of football. The players use their hands for tackling.

225

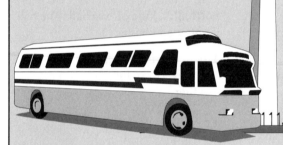

Around Town

  ## Performing Arts

Theater
Arena Stage
202/488-3300
Shakespeare Theatre
202/393-2700
Ford's Theatre
202/347-6262
National Theater
202/628-6161
Warner Theater
202/659-1600

**Washington Ballet
Company**
Oct, Dec, Feb, May,
at the Kennedy Center
202/362-3606

Washington Opera
November-March
at the Kennedy Center
202/416-7800

General Entertainment
Kennedy Center
202/416-8000
Wolf Trap Farm Park
703/255-1900

National Symphony Orchestra
September-May
at the Kennedy Center
202/467-4600

  ## Children's Events

Theater-in-the-Woods
May-September
703/255-1827

**Ringling Brothers and
Barnum and Bailey Circus**
Mid-April
202/432-7328 (Ticketmaster)

**National Theater
for Children**
October-April (Free)
202/783-3371

  ## Sports Events

Football
Washington Redskins
September-December
202/546-2222

Ice Hockey
Washington Capitals
October-April
301/350-3400

Basketball
Washington Bullets
November-April
301/350-3400

Golf
Kemper Open (PGA tour)
Mid-May
301/469-3737

Baseball
Baltimore Orioles
April-October
410/685-9800

Tennis
Washington Tennis Classic
Mid-July
703/276-4274

Performing Arts

In general, you can find out where to go and what is going on in:

- *The Washington Post*, especially the "Weekend" section on Fridays or the "Show" section on Sundays.
- *The Washington Times* "Weekend Magazine" on Thursdays.
- The *Washingtonian* magazine "Where & When" calendar.
- The Cultural Alliance directory. This lists most of the large and small theaters and concert halls; it is at many libraries. 202/638-2406
- Free weekly newspapers, such as the *City Paper,* which can be found in many stores, restaurants, and libraries.

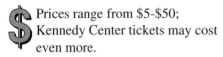 Prices range from $5-$50; Kennedy Center tickets may cost even more.

Discounts. You may get discounts for:

- groups of 15 or more.
- children and students (35% or more).
- senior citizens, 65 and older (15% or more).

Half-price tickets. You may get these at:

- some theaters on the day of the show. Call the theater and ask how to buy them.

- Ticketplace. Call 202/842-5387 for its new location and for information.

Theaters

Major theaters (see this chapter's opener for telephone numbers):

- Kennedy Center (Eisenhower Theater, Theater Lab). Musicals and first-run, well-known plays from New York. The smaller theaters in the Kennedy Center also have good productions—many for children. Check the newspaper for information on free programs, especially during holidays.
- Arena Stage. Both modern and classical plays.
- National Theater. Large productions—mostly musicals.
- Ford's Theatre. Plays—mostly musicals—for the whole family.
- Shakespeare Theatre. Shakespearean and other classical plays.
- Warner Theater. Mostly popular entertainment such as musicals.

Smaller theaters include:

- community theaters, found throughout the city and in many suburbs.
- college and university theaters. All colleges offer plays at different times of the year.
- experimental theaters, such as the Woolly Mammoth (202/393-3939) and the Studio (202/332-3300).

- dinner theaters (see chapter on "Dining In and Out").

International and foreign-language groups. The most famous of these is the Gala Hispanic Theater. For information about all foreign-language groups, read the Cultural Alliance Directory. 202/638-2406

Classical Music

The Kennedy Center. The main place for concerts, ballet, and opera is the Kennedy Center (see this chapter's opener for telephone numbers). You can get season tickets for many types of performances; that is, you pay one price for all the tickets in a season.

Museums. Concerts are regularly given at museums such as the:

- Smithsonian. 202/357-3030
- Phillips Collection. 202/387-0961

Concert Halls. Two of the larger concert halls are the:

- Lisner Auditorium at George Washington University. 202/994-1500
- DAR (Daughters of the American Revolution) Constitution Hall. 202/628-4780

Colleges. Almost all the colleges give concerts. For example, try:

- University of Maryland, College Park. Excellent music department. 301/405-5566

- George Mason University. Excellent music and drama series. 703/993-8888.
- Catholic University. The Washington Summer Opera has two productions starting in May. 202/526-1669

Washington National Cathedral. Mostly religious music; some free concerts. 202/537-6200

Outdoor theaters:

- Wolf Trap Farm Park, Filene Center. Operas, symphonies, ballets, and soloists. May–September. 703/255-1860. (Wolf Trap also has an indoor theater, The Barns at Wolf Trap. Open September-May. 703/938-2404)
- Carter-Barron Amphitheater. Some free concerts and plays. Open June-September. 202/426-6837

Private Art Galleries

Washington has over 100 private galleries where you can look at and buy art. Most of these galleries are free to visit. For special events, there may be a charge. To find out what each gallery has:

- Visit a gallery and look for the guide called *Galleries,* or call 202/667-1966.
- Check the "Weekend" sections of local newspapers.

Each gallery sets its own hours, usually 10 am-5 pm. Some are closed on Sundays or Mondays. Call for details.

Good areas to look for galleries are:

- around Dupont Circle in northwest Washington.
- Old Town Alexandria. Be sure to visit the Torpedo Factory, which has many galleries in an old building. 703/838-4565
- Georgetown.

Movies

 Most movie houses show each film three or four times a day, especially on weekends. The most popular times are the "early bird" (matinées before 6 pm) and the evening shows on Saturdays and Sundays.

 Most movie tickets cost $6-$7 a person. Many movie houses have special "early bird" prices; these are usually $3-$4. Children under 12 and senior citizens get discounts.

Foreign films. You can find these at the following theaters:

- Biograph, Georgetown. 202/333-2696
- Key, Georgetown. 202/333-5100
- American Film Institute at the Kennedy Center. 202/828-4000
- Outer Circle, upper Northwest, DC. 202/244-3116

- American University shows free movies Monday-Thursday. 202/885-2040
- The Washington, DC International Film Festival ("Filmfest DC "). Annual event in late April-early May. 202/727-2396

Sightseeing

 All of the sites on the Mall downtown are free, but you may pay a fee for some activities—such as special tours or movies.

 Most museums are open 10 am-5:30 pm every day. Summer hours are often longer.

Getting there

You can drive to the museums, but it is hard to find parking. The Metro stops near most major museums are:

- Smithsonian (blue and orange lines).
- Archives (yellow line).
- L'Enfant Plaza (blue, orange, yellow, and green lines).

Sites to see

The Smithsonian has about nine museums on the Mall and is the world's largest museum complex. Begin with the Information Center in the Castle, which has an orientation for visitors to the museum. For information on all the Smithsonian museums, call Dial-A-Museum. 202/ 357-2020

Some of the most popular museums are:

- National Air and Space Museum, which has movies about the history of flight on a huge screen.
- Museum of Natural History, famous for its jewels and dinosaurs.
- Museum of History and Technology, with its First Ladies' Hall.

The National Gallery of Art.

- the West Wing, with traditional art up to the early 20th century.
- the East Wing, with modern art collections.

Memorials.

- Washington Monument.
- Jefferson Memorial. Most popular during cherry blossom time (see Appendix A on "Washington, a Place to Live").
- Lincoln Memorial.
- Vietnam Veterans' Memorial.

Government buildings.

- White House.
- Capitol.
- Supreme Court.
- Federal Bureau of Investigation (FBI).
- National Archives.

Arlington National Cemetery has President Kennedy's grave.

The Holocaust Museum is the newest popular site. It is a memorial to the Jews and other victims of the Nazis during World War II. The museum opened in spring 1993. Call ahead of time to be sure you can get in. 202/488-0400

Tours

The Tourmobile. The blue and white Tourmobile bus goes to 18 major sites, including Arlington National Cemetery and the Kennedy Center. You can buy a ticket from the driver or at any of the booths on the mall.

The ride lasts about 1½ hours. You may get off at any site and look around for as long as you like. A bus stops at each site every 15-20 minutes.

 The Tourmobile goes 8:30 am-4:30 pm, 7 days a week.

 $8.50 for adults and $4.00 for children.

Museum tours. Most museums offer free tours with guides or self-guided tours on cassette tape; the museum gives out the headset, so you do not have to bring your own. Call to find out when you can take a guided tour in your language.

Many museums have written guides in other languages.

Special tours. You can get:

- chauffeured limousines for about $35-$55 per hour, plus tax and tip. Reserve at least 2 days in advance; tell the company what you want to see and which language you want the driver to speak.
- cruise ships for $18-$39.
- carriage rides for $40.
- mule-drawn canal boats along the C&O Canal for $2.50-$4.
- helicopter rides for $495 per hour.
- multi-lingual tours. Prices vary.

Fun for Children

Theaters

Special events. Many events are listed on this chapter's opener. Other events are:

- Adventure Theater, Glen Echo Park, MD. 301/320-5331
- BARNSTORM!, Barns of Wolf Trap Farm Park, has folk singers, and dancers, puppeteers, mimes, and storytellers. October-May. 703/255-1827
- Discovery Theater, the Smithsonian's Arts & Industries Building. 202/357-1300

The Zoo

The zoo is on Connecticut Avenue (Woodley Park/National Zoo or Cleveland Park stop, red line). It has over 5,000 kinds of animals; the most famous of these is the giant panda Hsing-Hsing from China.

 The Zoo is open every day—except for Christmas. The park is open until sunset. The hours for the buildings are:

- 9 am-6 pm, May 1- September 15.
- 9 am-4:30 pm, September 16- April 30.

Museums

Some of the museums especially for children are:

- the Capital Children's Museum. 202/543-8600
- the Discovery Room in the Museum of Natural History. 202/357-2020
- the National Aquarium. 202/377-2825
- the National Capital Trolley Museum. 301/384-6088

Sports Events

Cycling

World-famous cyclists come to the Tour DuPont race in mid-May. See *The Washington Post* in May for details.

Football

You probably will not be able to get tickets to see the Redskins, Washington's professional football team, but you can see the games every

Sunday or Monday night on TV. The season usually starts in September.

Horse racing

The most famous thoroughbred racing track is Pimlico Race Course in Baltimore. 301/542-9400

You can see harness-racing at the:

- Laurel Raceway. 301/725-0400
- Rosecroft Raceway in Oxon Hill, MD. 301/567-4005

Tennis

The two most important tournaments are the men's Washington Tennis Classic in July (see this chapter's opener) and the Women's Tennis Association Champions' Challenge in late August. Both events take place at the Washington Tennis Center, 16th & Kennedy Streets, NW. For more information, call the Tournament Hotline. 703/276-4274

Track

The Mobil 1 Invitational Track and Field Meet at George Mason University in mid-February is the main event. Get tickets early. 703/993-3270

Nightclubs

 Club hours are usually 9 pm-2 or 3 am on weekends; most clubs close earlier on week nights, but some are open until 2 am.

Legal age. The legal drinking age is 21. Many clubs ask for proof of your age at the door; bring a photo ID—such as a driver's license, a student ID, or a passport.

What to wear. A few clubs require men to wear a jacket and tie. Many clubs will not let you enter in jeans, sneakers (tennis shoes), or T-shirts.

Where to go. Most clubs are in the District—for example, in Adams Morgan and Georgetown. Some clubs are in the suburbs—for example, in Alexandria, VA, and Bethesda, MD. You can find nightclubs in every area of Washington.

Happy hours. Most bars have a "happy hour" after work (5–8 pm); during these hours, you can get free snacks and lower prices for certain drinks.

 The average "cover charge," or cost to enter, is about $5, but it can be as high as $20; some

---

For information on professional sports such as baseball, basketball, ice hockey, and golf, see this chapter's opener. Also see the "Sports" section of *The Washington Post*.

clubs have no cover charge. Alcoholic drinks cost $2-$5 each. Tip the waiter about 5%-10%.

⊗ Do not drive after you drink; the laws against drinking and driving are strict. In fact, sometimes the police set up checkpoints along the road; they may stop you and ask you to take a test for drunken driving. If you are "under the influence," you may pay a fine, lose your license, or even go to jail.

Words to Know

Checkpoints: places along the road where the police stop cars to check the drivers for drinking alcohol

Cover charge: the price you pay to enter a nightclub

Cruise ship: a sightseeing boat

Dinner theater: a combination theater and restaurant. You eat dinner first and then watch a play or musical from your table.

Drinking age: the legal age for buying and drinking alcohol

"Early bird": lower prices for movies shown in the afternoon

Happy hour: a time at a nightclub or restaurant when you can get free snacks and discounts on certain drinks

Mime: an actor who performs without speaking

Musical: a light play with singing

Nightclub: a place where you can listen to music, meet people, dance, and get food and drinks

Puppeteer: a person who moves dolls in a play, usually for children

Season ticket: a ticket or group of tickets for all the theater shows or sports games in a season

Nightclub

Spy Club. 805 15th St., NW, Washington, DC 20005. 202/289-1779. Dancing on Wed. & Thurs., 10 pm- 2 am; Sat., 9 pm-3 am.

Art gallery/ Classes

Rock Creek Gallery, The Art Barn Association. 2401 Tilden St., NW, Rock Creek Park, Washington, DC 20008. 202/244-2482. Gallery exhibiting artists living in the DC metro area. Fine arts & crafts. Open juried competitions; adult and child classes. Wed.-Sat., 10-5; Sun., 12-5.

__Dining In & Out__

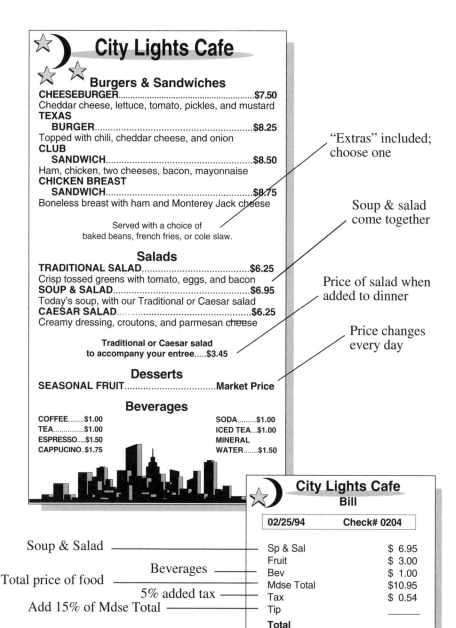

City Lights Cafe

Burgers & Sandwiches

CHEESEBURGER..$7.50
Cheddar cheese, lettuce, tomato, pickles, and mustard
TEXAS
  BURGER..$8.25
Topped with chili, cheddar cheese, and onion
CLUB
  SANDWICH..$8.50
Ham, chicken, two cheeses, bacon, mayonnaise
CHICKEN BREAST
  SANDWICH..$8.75
Boneless breast with ham and Monterey Jack cheese

Served with a choice of
baked beans, french fries, or cole slaw.

Salads

TRADITIONAL SALAD.......................................$6.25
Crisp tossed greens with tomato, eggs, and bacon
SOUP & SALAD...$6.95
Today's soup, with our Traditional or Caesar salad
CAESAR SALAD...$6.25
Creamy dressing, croutons, and parmesan cheese

Traditional or Caesar salad
to accompany your entree.....$3.45

Desserts

SEASONAL FRUIT..............................Market Price

Beverages

COFFEE........$1.00   SODA.........$1.00
TEA..............$1.00   ICED TEA...$1.00
ESPRESSO.....$1.50   MINERAL
CAPPUCINO..$1.75   WATER.......$1.50

"Extras" included;
choose one

Soup & salad
come together

Price of salad when
added to dinner

Price changes
every day

City Lights Cafe
Bill

02/25/94	Check# 0204

Sp & Sal	$ 6.95
Fruit	$ 3.00
Bev	$ 1.00
Mdse Total	$10.95
Tax	$ 0.54
Tip	_____
Total	_____

Soup & Salad
Beverages
Total price of food
5% added tax
Add 15% of Mdse Total

American Foods

Meals

Breakfast. Common breakfast foods are: cereal; toast, bagel, or muffins; eggs; bacon or breakfast sausage; waffles or pancakes; fruit juice (orange, grapefruit, or apple); coffee or tea.

A continental breakfast in a hotel or restaurant costs $5-$7. You get:

- juice.
- coffee or tea.
- rolls or muffins.

A full breakfast is usually about $10. A muffin and coffee in a coffee shop is usually $3-$5.

Lunch. The most popular time for lunch is 12 or 1 pm. Restaurants serve lunch from 11 am-3 pm. Most Americans eat a light and fast lunch, since lunch breaks last only 1 hour or less. Common lunch foods are sandwiches, salad, and soup. Lunch menus at restaurants are usually less expensive than dinner menus, but the amount of food you get is less, too. Lunch at a hotel is usually about $8-$15; you will pay $5-$8 for a sandwich and a drink at a quick restaurant.

Dinner. This is the largest meal of the day. In the U.S., most people eat dinner earlier than most Europeans and South Americans—about 6-7 pm.

Most restaurants serve dinner from 5-10 pm; restaurants in the suburbs and rural areas may close earlier.

Most dinners include a green salad, which is eaten before the meal; meat, chicken, or fish; cooked vegetables; and bread. Entrée prices vary widely, depending on the restaurant.

Some restaurants have "early-bird specials"—usually served around 6-7 pm, depending on the restaurant. The "early-bird specials" are cheaper than the later meals. Usually, you pay one price for a complete dinner.

Brunch. A brunch is one large meal for both breakfast and lunch—most popular on Sundays and holidays. Some restaurants serve a special Sunday brunch menu from 11 am-3 pm. Many of these brunches are buffets. At a buffet brunch, you go up to the food tables and fill your plate as many times as you want. Buffet brunches usually cost about $15-$30 per person.

Restaurants

The prices on the menu do not include tip or tax. Tip waiters about 15%-20% of the bill—before tax. Leave the tip on the table or add it to your bill.

Pay for the tax as part of the bill. Restaurant taxes are:

- DC: 9%.
- MD: 5%.
- VA : 4.5%.

Types of restaurants

Restaurants (full-service) range from informal to very formal (tie and jacket).

$ Prices in full-service restaurants vary from inexpensive ($5-$10 per person) to very expensive ($100 per person). The average cost per person in the city is $15-$30 for a meal and one soft drink.

Cafés, coffee shops, and diners serve coffee and pastries, in addition to breakfast and typical American meals. The price per person is about $5-$15 for lunch or dinner.

Cafeterias are self-service restaurants. You take a tray and move through a line, choosing the food you want. Pay at the cash register before you eat. Cafeterias are informal. The price per person is about $5-$10.

Delicatessens (delis) serve sandwiches, salads, and soups. Some have no tables or chairs—you have to take the food with you. Delis are informal. The price of a sandwich or salad is about $5-$8. "Gourmet" delis are usually more expensive.

Snack bars have snacks—such as potato chips, pretzels, and cookies—as well as fast foods and some sandwiches. Usually there are no chairs—just counters where you can stand while eating. Snack bars are very informal. Chips cost about 50¢; a hot dog costs $1-$2.

Fast-food restaurants serve food that is prepared quickly or made ahead of time—such as hamburgers and french fries. You order "for here" if you want to eat at the restaurant, or "to go" if you want to take the food somewhere else. The price of a full meal at most fast-food restaurants is about $4-$7.

Dinner theaters have food and entertainment including comedy, musicals, and mysteries. Dinner is served at a buffet or at your table.

Tickets ($25-$35 each) include entertainment and food, but not drinks, tax, and tip.

Dinner cruises have full-service meals aboard a boat as it cruises the Potomac River (the District or Old Town Alexandria) or the Chesapeake Bay (Baltimore). Make reservations at

---

Take-out and delivery lets you order food and eat it at home. With take-out restaurants, you pick the food up and take it home to eat; often, you can order ahead of time by telephone. Some restaurants deliver the food to you. Most Chinese restaurants and pizzerias have food to take out and delivery service. Pizza or Chinese food for two costs about $10-$15. Most delivery services are free if you order above their minimum price.

least 1-2 weeks in advance. Tickets ($40-$55) include food, but not drinks, tax, and tip.

Where to go

Washington, DC.

- Georgetown. A variety of formal and informal restaurants along M St. and Wisconsin Ave. and at Washington Harbor on K St.
- Adams Morgan. Many ethnic restaurants—ranging from Latin American to Ethiopian cuisine. This is a popular area at night and during the weekend. Located along 18th St. and Columbia Rd., NW.
- Dupont Circle. Over 100 restaurants within the radius of a mile.
- Chinatown. About 40 Chinese restaurants within just a few blocks of 6th and H Streets, NW.
- Union Station. A large food court, or open area, with many types of fast-food restaurants on the lower level; full-service restaurants on the main level (see chapter on "Shops & Malls").
- Post Office Pavilion, 1100 Pennsylvania Ave., NW. A food court and some full-service restaurants.

Virginia. One popular area is Old Town Alexandria, which has good seafood restaurants and ice-cream parlors, some with a river view. On Friday and Saturday nights, many of the stores in Old Town stay open.

Maryland. The place with the most restaurants in a small area is Bethesda, with many international restaurants.

How to dine

1. **Call ahead of time.**

Make a reservation if the restaurant is very popular—especially if you are going on a Friday or Saturday night. Many restaurants do not take reservations.

Ask about the parking. Is it self- or valet parking?

2. **Give your name to the host/ hostess or head waiter when you arrive.**

3. **Ask for the smoking or non-smoking section.**

Americans are much stricter about smoking laws than most other countries. By law, most restaurants must have a non-smoking area. If you sit there, you cannot smoke. A few restaurants do not allow smoking at all.

4. **Order.**

Usually, the waiter or waitress will take your drink order first. Water is free. Most restaurants offer courses *à la carte*—you can order the courses separately if you do not want a full-course dinner. Salad is usually offered as a first course.

5. **Pay the check (bill).**

In some American restaurants, the waiter or waitress gives you the check before you ask for it—sometimes even before you finish eating; you do not have to leave until you want to.

Many Americans share the cost of a meal when they are with friends—that is, they "split the bill," or divide it evenly. At most restaurants, each person in the group gives a credit card and the waiter puts the same amount on each person's bill. If each person wants to pay separately, tell the waiter ahead of time.

Entertaining At Home

Caterers

Ready-made. Many gourmet delis, restaurants, hotels, supermarkets, and catering services prepare food platters for parties. You can pick up the food or have it delivered.

Buying prepared platters is cheaper than ordering a custom menu or hiring a full catering service (see below). Prices depend on the type and quantity of food ordered. For example, a deli platter (cold meats and cheeses) for 20 people can be about $60-$130.

Prepared in your home. You can hire a caterer to prepare and serve a custom-made menu in your home. Most caterers will also help you plan the menu. Some services provide their own dishes, serving pieces, tablecloths, napkins, and decorations.

Catered food costs about $15-$35 per person. Some caterers bring a private chef. The cost is $20-$30 an hour extra.

Other services

Bartenders (for preparing and serving drinks). Most charge about $15-$20 an hour, per bartender, for a minimum of 4-5 hours. You can find bartenders through professional services or bartending schools. Some services can provide the drinks, but it is usually cheaper to buy your own beer, wine, and liquor at a liquor store.

Maid and butler service (for serving food and cleaning after the party). Most charge about $20-$30 an hour, per server, for a minimum of 3-5 hours. If you have a housekeeper, he or she may be willing to help you serve and/or clean.

Party-planning services plan the whole party—from food and decorations to entertainment. Prices vary greatly, depending on the service.

Parking attendants provide valet parking for your guests. The average cost is $20 an hour, per attendant, for a minimum of 4 hours. Ask for insurance, in case the attendants damage one of the cars.

241

Words to Know

À la carte: a menu with a separate price for each item

Bartender: a person who makes and serves alcoholic and soft drinks

Brunch: one large meal for breakfast and lunch together

Buffet: a meal where you serve yourself

Cafeteria: a restaurant where you serve yourself and take your food to a table

Cater: to provide food for a party. Caterers cook or bake for you.

Continental breakfast: a breakfast with juice, coffee or tea, and rolls or muffins

Counter: a long table where you sit and eat your food

Course: one part of a meal—for example, the appetizer or dessert

Delicatessen (deli): a restaurant with sandwiches, salads, and soups

"Early-bird" special: a meal served early in the evening—at a lower price

Entrée: main course

Fast-food: food made and served quickly—such as McDonald's hamburgers

Food court: an area in a mall or shopping center with many types of fast-food restaurants

"For here": food you eat in the restaurant

Gourmet: special food—usually tastier than ordinary food

Platter: a large plate with meats, cheeses, fruit, or desserts

Reservation: a time when a restaurant saves a table for you

Take-out: food you get at the restaurant and then take home to eat

"To go": food you take out of the restaurant

Valet parking: personal parking. Someone takes your car when you arrive at the restaurant or party and gets it for you when you leave.

PLATO'S PALATE

CARRY OUT GRILL

SPECIALIZING IN
* HOMEMADE GREEK DAILY SPECIALS
* CHARBROILED BURGERS
* OVERSTUFFED SUBS AND SANDWICHES
* HOMEMADE DESSERTS
* PIZZA

HOURS:
MONDAY-FRIDAY
7 A.M. — 9 P.M.
SATURDAY
9 A.M. — 9 P.M.

"HOME OF THE OUZO BURGER"

7639 OLD GEORGETOWN ROAD, BETHESDA, MD
(301) 907-2969

MOUSSAKA * PASTICHIO * DOLMADES * SPANAKOPITA * LAMB KAPAMA * YOUVETSI

243

Traveling In & Out
of the U.S.

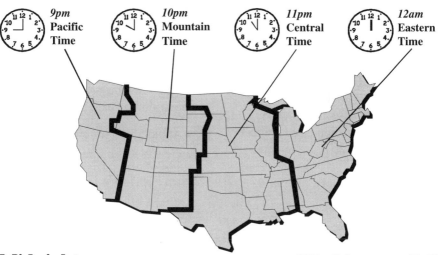

9pm Pacific Time

10pm Mountain Time

11pm Central Time

12am Eastern Time

Midnight ——————————— Washington, DC

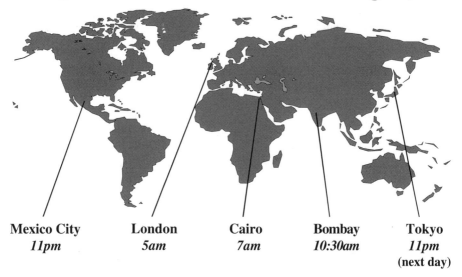

Mexico City
11pm

London
5am

Cairo
7am

Bombay
10:30am

Tokyo
11pm
(next day)

Getting Ready

Leaving the country

Your passport. Make a photocopy of your passport. Carry it separately in case the passport is lost or stolen.

Before you leave:

- Check your visa status. Your visa shows if you can get into the U.S. again (see chapter on "Your Legal Status").
- Find out if you need new entry papers. For example, anyone with a J-1 visa may need another IAP-66 (pink form) to re-enter the country.
- Inform the school's international students' office if you are a student.

Money

Traveler's checks. Get them from your bank, an American Express office, or a foreign exchange office.

A major credit card. Write down the number of your credit card in case it is lost or stolen. Carry it separately from your credit cards.

ATM (automatic teller machine) bank card. You may use an ATM in most areas of the U.S.

Travel insurance

You may buy travel insurance from:

- travel agents.
- health insurance companies.
- travel insurance companies.

Trip cancellation or interruption insurance is for emergencies. For example, you may have to cancel your trip because of an emergency—such as the illness or death of a family member. Cancellation/interruption insurance will give you back any fees you have already paid for the trip.

 About $5-$6 for every $100 of coverage.

Medical assistance insurance is for accidents or illnesses that happen on the trip. Check with your insurance company to see if you are already insured while traveling; ask what you should do if you need to see a doctor in another area of the U.S. or in another country.

 The average cost of medical insurance for a 15-day trip is $75 for a family, $50 for an individual.

⊗ When you arrive, put any valuables—such as jewelry, camera equipment, airplane tickets, and extra money—in a hotel

---

Get flight and hotel reservations as soon as you can—especially if you are traveling during the holidays. Confirm all reservations before you leave.

---

safe-deposit box. Never leave your camera in the room—always carry it with you. Be especially careful in large cities and on beaches. Do not let go of the valuables you carry, anywhere—even for a minute.

How to leave your home

1. **Arrange for someone to take care of your home.**

Have a friend or neighbor watch your house or apartment while you are away. It is not impolite to ask someone who lives close to you—even if you do not know that person very well.

Keep lights on at all times or use a timer that turns the lights on or off; you can get a timer at a hardware store. Close all curtains and blinds.

2. **Ask your newspaper carriers and post office to hold deliveries while you are away.**

For short trips, ask a neighbor to pick up your newspaper and mail every day.

3. **Get a petsitter or take your pets to a kennel.**

A petsitter is a person who comes to your home and takes care of your pets while you are away.

4. **Unplug all heating appliances if you will be away for a long time.**

This will protect your appliances from fire. Do not unplug your refrigerator.

5. **Tell the neighbors you will be away.**

Ask them to call the police or fire department in case of emergency or if they see a stranger near your house. Leave a phone number where they can reach you.

Getting There
Cars

American highways are usually fast and well-kept. When you plan your trip, try to stay away from big cities during the rush hours. If traffic is light, you can get to:

- New York City: 4½-5 hours.
- Philadelphia: 2½-3 hours.
- Boston: 9 hours.
- Atlanta: 12 hours.

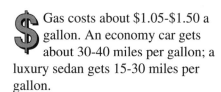 Gas costs about $1.05-$1.50 a gallon. An economy car gets about 30-40 miles per gallon; a luxury sedan gets 15-30 miles per gallon.

On major highways, you will pay tolls; most are 50¢-$2 each. Tolls from Washington, DC, to New York City are $10-$12.

Renting a car. You must be at least 21 years old to rent a car.

You will need an International Driver's License and a license from your home country.

 Prices vary according to the type of car and the company. These are some average prices per day:

- subcompact: $30.
- sedan: $40.
- luxury: $70.

Gasoline. The car you get will have a full tank of gas. If you do not return it with a full tank, you pay for the gas you used. The price per gallon is often higher than the price at a gas station.

Insurance. Get car insurance if necessary. First check with your car insurance company to see if you need extra insurance; you can buy this insurance from the car rental agency for $1.50-$13 a day.

Bus

Taking a bus is usually less expensive than other forms of travel, but buses often take longer because they stop in many places. Call and ask about express (nonstop) service.

The most popular bus company for long-distance travel is Greyhound-Trailways; the station is located in downtown Washington (see "Information"). The bus line also has information in Spanish (see "Information").

 The cost of some round trips from Washington, DC, are:

- $50 to New York City.
- $84 to Boston.
- $135.50 to Chicago.

Some bus companies have special discount programs. For example, Greyhound-Trailways has an Ameripass program that lets you travel all over the country at a discount.

Train

Amtrak is the only train that goes from the Washington area to other parts of the country. All trains have a café or dining car; some have sleeping cars. The three Amtrak stations in the Washington area are:

- Union Station in the District.
- New Carrollton in Prince George's County, MD.
- Alexandria in Fairfax County, VA.

Amtrak has a:

- regular train.
- Metroliner. The Metroliner is faster and costs more. You must reserve your seat in advance or get tickets in the station before you get on the train.

The Metroliner is usually on time—even in bad weather; the regular train is late more often. Sample trip times on the Metroliner are:

- 2 hours to Philadelphia.
- 2½-3 hours to New York City.
- 8 hours to Boston.

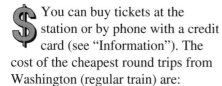 You can buy tickets at the station or by phone with a credit card (see "Information"). The cost of the cheapest round trips from Washington (regular train) are:

- $89 to New York City.
- $128 to Boston.
- $125 to Chicago.

If you want to tour the East Coast by train, find out about Amtrak's discount passes, which include:

- 45-day passes for the East Coast.
- the International USA Railpass for international visitors and residents.

Plane

Buying the tickets. The Washington area has three main airports (see chapter on "When You Arrive").

You can buy tickets through a travel agent or directly from an airline. Get the tickets as soon as you can; you may get discounts for advance purchase. Before you buy the tickets, find out if they are refundable, or if you can cancel the flight and get your money back.

You can take a shuttle from Washington to New York City. The shuttle runs every hour; you do not have to reserve your flight in advance. Call US Air or Delta Air Lines for information.

 Some round-trip coach (least expensive) prices from Washington, DC are:

- $160-$250 to New York City.
- $250 to Boston.
- $200-$350 to Chicago.
- $400-$450 to Los Angeles.

The airport

 Allow extra time to get to the airport if you are traveling around the time of a major holiday—especially if you are leaving from National Airport. Plan to arrive at the airport terminal at least:

- 2 hours before departure time for international flights.
- 1 hour before departure time for domestic flights.

Baggage. Call the airline ahead of time and ask:

- how many bags you can take.
- how much the bags can weigh.
- how big the bags can be.

Transportation (see chapter on "When You Arrive" for ways to get to the airport).

Parking. If you drive to the airport, you can park your car in a long-term parking lot for $8-$10 per day. A shuttle bus will take you from the parking lot to the airport terminal for free.

Where to Stay

Hotels often have rooms, food, and personal services—such as room service, laundry, and transportation to and from airports. Some hotels have sports and fitness centers, tour services, and night clubs. Costs vary; the average cost for a double (two-person) hotel room in major cities is $60-$200 per night.

Motels and motor lodges have bedrooms with bathrooms and parking. Many also have restaurants, kitchenettes, washers and dryers, and pools. The average cost for a double room is $30-$80 per night.

Bed & Breakfasts (B&Bs) have bedrooms with private or shared bathrooms, usually in old houses or historic buildings. These inns are often small and cozy and are run by a family or individual. The average for a double room is $50-$150 per night, breakfast included.

House, condominium, and cabin rentals usually have most furnishings—bed linens, towels, dishes, and kitchen utensils, but you may have to rent for 1 week or more. Prices vary.

American Youth Hostels are for travelers of all ages (see "Information"). Usually, you share a bedroom and bathroom with other people. The cost per night is about $7-$20; you pay extra for bedding, towels, or meals. Members get discounted rates; membership fees are $15-$35 per year.

Camping is popular in national parks. Some camping facilities have cooking grills, toilets, and showers. Some campsites are free; others charge a fee of $8-$10.

Information

Travel

AMTRAK: 1-800-USA-RAIL

Greyhound-Trailways Bus Lines: 202/565-2662. *En Español*: 1-800/531-5332

Places to stay

American Youth Hostels.

- DC or VA: 202/783-4943
- MD: 301/209-8544

National Park Service: 202/208-4747

Weather

Weather Reports (2,000 U.S. and foreign cities; 75¢ a minute): 1-900-HI-OR-LO

General Weather Information (all U.S. states, except Hawaii and Alaska): 703/260-0107

Words to Know

Advance purchase: buying tickets in advance, or ahead of time

Airline: a company that owns and flies airplanes—such as TWA, Delta Air Lines, or British Airways

Long-term parking lot: a place near the airport where you can park your car for more than one day

Medical assistance insurance: insurance that pays for your medical care during a trip

Motel: a kind of hotel. Each room has a door to the outside and comes with a parking space.

Round trip: a trip that takes you somewhere and brings you back again

Shuttle: a flight that goes every hour. You do not have to reserve it.

Shuttle bus: a bus that takes you back and forth, as from the parking lot to the main part of the airport

Toll: money paid for using some roads and bridges

Trip cancellation insurance: insurance that pays for your trip if you cannot go or have to come home

Youth hostel: a place to stay while you are on a trip. Usually, you share a bedroom and bathroom with other people.

Holidays &
Special Events

Call 202/737-8866 to listen to a recorded listing of the week's special events. Visit or call the Washington Visitor's Center at 202/789-7038 for a calendar of events.

 New Years Day* **(January 1):** New Year's Eve (Dec. 31) family celebrations in Leesburg, VA and Annapolis, MD. Local restaurants and clubs offer special dinner parties.

Chinese New Year Parade: Marching bands, dragon and lion dancers, clowns, and other entertainers. 1:00 pm along H St. in Chinatown. 202/638-1041

Washington Antiques Show: Antique collections, lectures, and tours. 202/234-0700

Martin Luther King, Jr. Day* **(2nd Monday):** Honors the civil rights leader. Ceremony at the Lincoln Memorial with King's famous "I Have a Dream" speech.

 St. Valentine's Day **(February 14):** Honors the people we love. Many give cards and gifts to special friends and family members.

President's Day* **(3rd Monday):** Honors the birthdays of Presidents Lincoln and Washington. Parade in Alexandria, VA. Ceremony at Washington's tomb in Mt. Vernon, VA. 10-kilometer road race in Alexandria on the Saturday before the holiday.

Ramadan: A month of fasting, starting in February. Ending with the Eide Al-fetter festival, with a breakfast and celebration at area mosques and the Islamic Center.

Black History Month: Special programs in museums and schools celebrate African-American history and culture.

Washington Boat Show: Sailboats and power boats. The Washington Convention Center, 9th and H Sts., NW. 703/569-7141

 St. Patrick's Day **(March 17):** Honors an Irish saint. Parade on Constitution Ave. between 7th and 17th Sts. on the Sunday before March 17. Irish people wear green.

Washington Flower & Garden Show: Over 10,000 flowers. The

Washington Convention Center, 9th and H Sts. 703/569-7141

Smithsonian Kite Festival: Kite-flying competitions on the Mall at the Washington Monument. 202/357-3030

 Easter (March or April): Easter Sunrise Service at Arlington National Cemetery in VA. Easter Egg Roll contest at the White House for children age 8 and younger.

Cherry Blossom Festival (early April): Week when Washington's cherry blossom trees bloom. Parade and the lighting of a 300-year-old Japanese stone lantern. 202/619-7222

 Eide Hijja: Holy day when many Muslims make pilgrimage to Mecca. Festival and prayers at area mosques and the Islamic Center.

Mother's Day (2nd Sunday): Honors mothers. Many give cards and gifts to their mothers.

Memorial Day* (last Monday): Honors soldiers killed in war. Special evening concert on the West Lawn of the U.S. Capitol on the evening before Memorial Day.

Asian Pacific American Heritage Festival: Freedom Plaza, 1300 Pennsylvania Ave., NW. 301/258-5095

Chesapeake Bay Bridge Walk: 4.3-mile walk across the eastbound span of the Bay Bridge. 410/288-8405

 Father's Day (3rd Sunday): Honors fathers. Many give cards and gifts to their fathers.

Philippine Independence Day: Parade on Pennsylvania Ave. and a fair at Freedom Plaza, 1300 Pennsylvania Ave., NW. 202/483-1414

Smithsonian Folklife Festival: Celebration of the nation's different folk/ethnic cultures, with music, dance, ethnic foods, crafts, and other activities. The Mall. 202/357-2700

 Independence Day* **(July 4):** Celebrates U.S. independence from England. Festivities all day on the Mall. Independence Day Parade. Concerts on the West Lawn of the U.S. Capitol and at the Lincoln Memorial. Fireworks at 9:15 pm.

Bastille Day (July 14): French Independence Day. Race of waiters and waitresses, live entertainment. 1900 Pennsylvania Ave., NW. 202/452-1126

Caribbean Summer in the Park: Caribbean music, food, and crafts. RFK Stadium. 301/249-1028

Latin American Festival: Latin American music, food, dance, and crafts. The Mall near the Washington Monument. 202/269-0101

Arlington County Fair: Exhibits, vendors, games, and carnival rides. Thomas Jefferson Community Center, 3501 2nd St., Arlington, VA. 703/ 358-6412

Montgomery County Fair: Country music, dancing, crafts, carnival rides, and livestock exhibits. The fairgrounds on Rte. 355, Gaithersburg, MD. 301/926-3100

Thai Heritage Festival: National Museum of Natural History. 202/786-2069

 Labor Day* (1st Monday): Honors workers. Concert on the evening before Labor Day, on the West Lawn of the U.S. Capitol.

Rosh Hashanah and Yom Kippur (end of September or beginning of October): Jewish New Year. Some schools and businesses are closed.

African Cultural Festival: African music, food, and crafts. Freedom Plaza, 1300 Pennsylvania Ave., NW. 202/667-5775

Adams-Morgan Day: Food, music, and crafts from Latin America, Africa, and Europe. 18th St., NW between Florida Ave. and Columbia Rd. 202/332-3292

Kalorama House and Embassy Tour: Tours of historic homes and embassies in the Kalorama neighborhood. 202/387-4062

Cathedral Open House: Demonstrations by master carvers, music, dancers, and tours. National Cathedral, Wisconsin and Massachusetts Aves., NW. 202/537-6200

 Columbus Day* (2nd Monday): Celebrates the discovery of America. Ceremonies at Union Station.

Halloween (October 31): "Fun" evening for children. Children go "trick-or-treating" or visit neighbors' homes and ask for a "treat."

The Capital Regatta: A sailboat race, which can be watched from the waterfront. 202/488-8980

Taste of DC: Music, dance, performances, and foods from several restaurants. Pennsylvania Ave. between 9th and 14th Sts. 202/724-2640

Washington International Horse Show: Competition among hundreds of horses and riders. Capital Centre, Landover, MD. 301/840-0281

Marine Corps Marathon: 26-mile race starting at the Iwo Jima memorial in Arlington, VA and passing through the District. 703/690-3431

 Veteran's Day* (November 11): Honors U.S. soldiers. Ceremonies at Arlington National Cemetery and at the Vietnam Veterans Memorial.

Thanksgiving Day* (3rd Thursday): Day for giving thanks for all we have. Families eat a special turkey dinner. Parade begins at 13th St. & Pennsylvania Ave., NW.

 Hanukkah (end of December): Jewish holiday that lasts 8 days. Many stores, homes, and public places have menorahs (candlesticks with eight branches).

Christmas* (December 25): Christian holiday. Lighting of the National Christmas Tree ceremony on the Ellipse (the park behind the White House) in mid-December. Special White House tours to view its Christmas decorations. Free holiday concerts at the Kennedy Center throughout December.

*On national holidays, all government offices, schools, and some businesses are closed.

Climate

Average Temperature in Washington, D.C. (°C)

Month	Jan	Feb	Mar	April	May	Jun	Jul	Aug	Sept	Oct	Nov	Dec
Average	3	3	8	13	19	24	26	25	21	15	9	3

Average Temperature in Washington, D.C. (°F)

Month	Jan	Feb	Mar	April	May	Jun	Jul	Aug	Sept	Oct	Nov	Dec
Average	37.4	37.4	46.4	55.4	66.2	75.2	78.8	77	69.8	59	48.2	37.4

°F → °C

- subtract 32 from °F
- multiply by 5
- divide by 9

[(N-32) x 5/9 = °C]

°C → °F

- multiply °C by 9
- divide by 5
- add 32

Weather information
24-hour recorded update
(no area code) 936-1212

_____Religions_____

Major religions in the Washington area have a referral service. If your religion is not listed, call individual places of worship listed in the phone book.

Buddist Temple
(202) 829-2423

Catholic Information Center
Archdiocese of Washington
(202) 783-2062

Bahai Faith Washington Center
(202) 291-5532

Episcopal: Diocese of Washington,
Prince Georges, Montgomery,
Charles, St. Mary's Counties,
District of Columbia
(202) 537-6560

Episcopal Diocese of Virginia
(703) 824-1198

Friends Meeting of Washington
(202) 483-3310

Hindu Temple of Washington
(202) 434-1000

Islamic Center
(202) 332-8343

Jewish Information and
Referral Service
(301) 770-4848

Korean Ministries Council
of Greater Washington
(703) 354-9223

Lutheran Synod
(202) 543-8610

Presbyterian District Superintendent
(301) 589-8772

Unitarian Universalist
Office of Social Concerns
(202) 547-0254

Measurements

American & Metric Systems

	American	Metric
Length	1 inch (1")	2.54 centimeters
	1 foot (1')	0.305 meter
	1 yard	0.914 meter
	1 mile	1.609 kilometers
Area	1 square inch	6.452 sq. cm.
	1 square foot	929.030 sq. cm.
	1 square yard	0.836 sq. m.
	1 acre	4,047 sq. m.
Volume/Capacity		
	1 pint	0.473 liter
	1 quart	0.946 liter
	1 gallon	3.785 liters
Weight	1 ounce	28.350 grams
	1 pound	453.592 grams
	1 ton	0.907 metric ton

	Metric	American
Length	1 centimeter	0.394 inch
	1 decimeter	03.937 inches
	1 meter	39.37 inches
	1 kilometer	0.621 mile
Area	1 square cm.	0.155 sq. in.
	1 centare	10.764 sq. ft.
	1 hectare	2.477 acres
Volume/Capacity		
	1 deciliter	0.211 pint
	1 liter	1.057 quarts
	1 decaliter	2.642 gallons
Weight	1 decagram	0.353 ounce
	1 kilogram	2.205 pounds
	1 metric ton	1.102 tons

American Money

With $1.00 you can:
- buy one large chocolate chip cookie
- buy one metrobus token

With $5.00 you can:
- rent two videos for a night
- dry clean a pair of pants

With $10.00 you can:
- pump a full tank of gas in a compact car
- get a quick haircut

With $20.00 you can:
- hire a babysitter (4 hrs)
- buy a fancy silk tie

With $50.00 you can:
- buy a pair of sneakers
- hire a maid (5 hrs)

With $100.00 you can:
- see a popular musical at the Kennedy Center with a friend

Tipping

Occupation	Average Amount to Tip
Restaurants	
waiters/waitresses	15% of food bill
(except for employees at "fast-food" restaurants)	not including tax
Airports, Trains, or Bus terminals	
baggage handlers–porters who carry	
your luggage	$1.00-$2.00 per bag
Barber shops/Beauty salons	
hairdressers and barbers	15%
Taxis and Limos	
drivers	10-15% of fare
Hotels	
room service (delivering food or laundry)	50¢ - $1.00
porters	$1.00 per bag
doorkeeper (who calls a taxi for you)	25-50¢

Do not tip:

■ **officials** such as police officers or government employees.

■ **service employees** such as bus drivers, theatre ushers, museum guides, sales people, gas station attendants, elevator operators, receptionists.

___Books to Read___

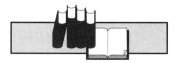

The Best of Washington, D.C. Bates, Colleen and Fisher, Robert, ed. New York: Prentice Hall, 1990.

Country Walks Near Washington. Alan Fischer. Baltimore: Appalachian Mountain Club. 410/ 523-5257

Cultural Alliance Directory: A Guide to Washington Area Artists and Cultural Organizations. Eisenberg, Karen, ed. Washington, D.C.: Cultural Alliance of Greater Washington, 1990.

The Dog Owner's Guide. Burger, Irene and Rand, Mary. Riverdale, Maryland: Edington-Rand, 1993. 301/ 779-7930

*Every*body's *Guide to the Law.* Belli, Marvin. Washington, D.C.: Harper & Row, 1987.

Export Programs: A Business Directory of U.S. Government Resources. Washington, D.C.: U.S. Department of Commerce, 1992.

Federal Personnel Guide. Chevy Chase, Maryland: Key Communications Group, 1993. 301/656-0450

Fifty Maps of Washington, D.C. Chaffee, Kevin, ed. New York: H.M. Gousha, 1991.

Finding Fun & Friends in Washington: An Uncommon Guide to Com-

mon Interests. Gottesman, Roberta. Alexandria, Virginia: Piccolo Press, 1992.

Finding a Job in the United States. Bradley, Curtis H. and Friedenberg, Joan E. Lincolnwood, Illinois: Passport Books, 1992.

How to Get a Federal Job. Chevy Chase, Maryland: Key Communications Group, 7th edition. 301/656-0450

Independent School Guide: Washington, D.C. and Surrounding Area. Chevy Chase, Maryland: Lois H. Coerper, Shirley W. Mersereau, 1991.

Literary Washington: A Complete Guide to the Literary Life in the Nation's Capital. Cutler, David. Lanham, Maryland: Madison Books, 1989.

Mastering D.C.: A Newcomers Guide to Living in Washington. Nowitz, Sheryl. Arlington, Virginia: Adventures Publishing, 1992.

The Metropolitan Job Bank: The Job Hunters Guide to Washington, D.C. Smith, Carter. Holbrook, Massachusetts: Bob Adams, Inc., 1992.

The Metropolitan Washington Preschool and Daycare Guidebook.

Washington, D.C.: The Preschool Book. 202/338-7257

Natural Washington. Berman, Richard and Gerhard, Deborah. McLean, Virginia: EPM Publications, 1991.

On the Spot:Pinpointing the Past In Washington, D.C. Evelyn, Douglas and Dickson, Paul. Washington, D.C.: Farragut Publishing Co., 1992. 202/872-4703

The Preschool & Daycare Guide. Cavanaugh, Merry. Washington, D.C. : Merry M. Cavanaugh, 1989.

Station Masters: A Comprehensive Pocket Guide to Metrorail Station Neighborhoods. Arlington, Virginia: Bowring Cartographic, 1988.

Summer Fun! A Guide to Camps in Greater Washington. Bethesda, Maryland: The Harbor School Parents' Association, 1992.

Washington Area Health and Fitness Guide. Heard, Ellen. Haras Salochin Press. Chevy Chase, MD , 1993. 301/ 946-1998

Washington Area Restaurants. Shirhall, Jean. Washington, D.C.: Center for the Study of Services, 1992.

Washington, D.C. Access, Wurman, Richard. New York: Access Press, 1992.

Washington, D.C.: The Complete Guide. Duffield, Kramer and Sheppard. New York: Vintage Books, 1991.

Washington, D.C. Guidebook for Kids. Noodle Press.

Washington, D.C. Museums: A Ross Guide. Ross, Betty. Chevy Chase, Maryland: Americana Press.   301/ 718-9808

The Washington Ethnic Bakery Guide. Lawson, Jim C. Washington, D.C. : Ardmore Publications, 1989.

The Washington Ethnic Food Store Guide. Lawson, Jim C. Washington, D.C. : Ardmore Publications, 1989.

Washington on Foot: 24 Walking Tours of Washington, D.C., Old Town Alexandria, Historic Annapolis. Brown, Lin and Protopappas, John, ed. Washington, D.C.: Smithsonian Institution Press, 1989.

The Washington Physicians Directory. Silver Spring, Maryland: National Directories, Inc., 1992.

Zagat Washington, D.C. Restaurant Survey. Boikess, Olga, ed. New York: Zagat Survey, 1991.

___Content Experts___

Susan Bellinger
VP, Business Development
Ruesch International

Bill Boddicker
Insurance Agent
State Farm Insurance

Shawny Burns
Public Relations & Fashion Director
Saks Fifth Avenue

Tristram Carlisle
Credit Officer
First American Bank

C. Elizabeth Espin Stern, Esq.
Immigration & International
   Employment Attorney
Shaw, Pittman, Potts & Trowbridge

Lewis R. Flax, VP
Westex Trade Services

Fred Gray, President
Pro-Line Security Systems

Dorit Jaffe
Advertising Coordinator
Giant Food Inc.

Dennis Kleban, M.D.
Allergist

Betty Loeb, CRS
Real Estate Agent
Long & Foster

Bernice W. Munsey, Ed.D.
Educational Counselor

Special thanks to:

Alan Alper, A.T., C., Ms.T.
Ralph Frisbee
David F. Gage
Helen Hillstrom, CRB, CRS, GRI
John E. Hopkinson, CPE, CFA
Ethna Hopper

Martin Kossoff, O.D.
Kim Lopes
Bonnie R. Ross
Richard Saah
Everett Schneider, D.D.S.
Shane Sharareh, CPA, MBA

Index of Advertisers

Index

Maps

Illustrations